A DIAMOND
in the
MASTER'S
HANDS

A DIAMOND
in the
MASTER'S HANDS

From ORDINARY *to* EXTRAORDINARY:
A JOURNEY *of* UNEARTHING
the TREASURE WITHIN

Lisa Neifert

XULON ELITE

Xulon Press Elite
555 Winderley Pl, Suite 225
Maitland, FL 32751
407.339.4217
www.xulonpress.com

Paperback ISBN-13: 978-1-66289-269-1
Ebook ISBN-13: 978-1-66289-270-7

ENDORSEMENTS

"I highly recommend this inspirational book. I was privileged to watch the Lord transform Mike and Lisa into the diamonds that they are today. This book will inspire you to follow your destiny in Christ."

Pastor Bill Breon
Senior Pastor of Ruslin Hills Church

"Over the past 30 years, it has been breathtaking to watch the wonder of God's work in and through Lisa. Lisa is an avid student of God's person, word and ways. Her godly zeal stirs up (and challenges) the spirits of all those fortunate enough to be around her.

This book chronicles Lisa's tenacious walk with the Lord and His great faithfulness to her. Her journey both inspires and comforts those pressing in for the abundant life Jesus promises. She has personally learned how to get free of spiritual bondages and to then walk out her inheritance in Jesus. She is always firmly set on a trajectory to grow in faith.

Lisa's story is one of hope for every person seeking to know God and their personal destiny in Him!"

Vivian Alderfer
Founder of Set Free to Set Free, Inc.

"It is my high honor to endorse my dear friend, Lisa Neifert's book, "A Diamond In The Father's Hand." Lisa and her husband Michael are not only cherished friends but extended family and it has been a JOY to see firsthand the testimony of trials and triumph throughout their lives. Lisa is wise beyond her years and she has given me insight that stretched me in my ministry and helped me discover some nuggets found only in digging deeper with our Lord. This book that you hold in your hand is an author whose sole desire is to honor God's heart. We have ministered together across America and multiple countries and their marriage and ministry has blessed me, my family and countless others.

Mike and Lisa today are a powerful couple for Christ and where they at times were broken and bound the Lord is now using them to bring freedom to those still stuck. They went from deep discouragement and near divorce to helping folks delivered and living life to the full. Lisa never gave up on her husband just like our Heavenly Father never gave up on us. Her prayers and persistence not only paid off but through each passing page reveal God's unceasing love for the world. Just like she didn't give up on her man because she has a Heavenly Father that hasn't given up on mankind. This book will be a game changer for some and life changer for others. I would encourage you to buy one for yourself and three others to give away! I am drawn closer to Christ because of their faith and His faithfulness. This book is not only well written but well lived. Well done my friend and praise the Lord!"

Frank Shelton, Jr.
Founder of Frank Shelton GLOBAL
Author - "Blessedness of Brokenness, Carrying Greatness
& URGENCY"

Former DC, MD & DE State Coordinator @ Billy Graham Evangelistic Assoc
Evangelism Chairman of 2012, 2016, 2020 & 2024 Olympics outreach
Host of BY FAITH radio & TV Ministry
FrankShelton.com - Waldorf, MD

"In my early years as a pastor, navigating the complexities of ministry in my 30s, the profound influence of Mike and Lisa catalyzed a transformative era for both myself and my wife. Their ministry illuminated the depths of a father's love, a concept previously ungrasped by us in its entirety. The essence of their spirit and boundless compassion mirrors this divine love, offering a reflection of the Heavenly Father's embrace.

As I delve into the pages of this book, Lisa's voice resonates with striking clarity. It's a harmonious blend of divine wisdom, infused with abundant humor and infectious laughter, all emanating from a heart deeply connected to the Father. This narrative isn't just words on a page; it's a testament to a life lived in close communion with God's spirit.

Prayer is the heartbeat of Mike and Lisa's life, a thread that weaves through every aspect of their existence. Much like this book, punctuated with moments of prayer, their daily lives are a testament to their unwavering faith, entrusting every detail and every moment to God's guidance and providence. This ceaseless devotion to prayer is not only inspiring but also a fundamental pillar of their spiritual journey.

Lisa's poignant testimonies have touched the hearts of my congregation, particularly resonating with wives navigating marital challenges. Her stories have sown seeds of hope and transformation, fostering a profound sense of solace and understanding.

Now, as I find myself in my late 40s, the friendship and spiritual kinship we share with Mike and Lisa continue to be a profound blessing. Their presence and guidance have been an immeasurable gift to both my marriage and our ministry, enriching our lives in countless ways.

This book is not merely a recounting of events; it's a journey through the evolution of their faith. It chronicles how, through unwavering belief and trust in the Almighty, they have witnessed God releasing outrageous wonders. It's a story of faith maturing in the face of life's trials, a testament to the awe-inspiring work of God in everyday lives."

Cyril Petit
Senior Pastor of Église Baptiste Emmanuel, France

A DIAMOND IN THE
MASTER'S HANDS

FROM ORDINARY TO EXTRAORDINARY: A JOURNEY OF UNEARTHING THE
TREASURE WITHIN

Stephanie, Michael, Ashley, Steven, Samantha, me and Mike

DEDICATION

To my fearless husband and best friend, Mike, for giving me the priceless opportunity to stay home raising our three beautiful children. Thank you for your love, patience, and encouragement to pen this book. I am forever grateful to you for reminding me to go for the "big cup" and cheering me on. I am so proud to be your wife and honored to do life with you. I am truly spoiled. I thank God as we celebrate our 40th wedding anniversary this year! I love you.

To my children Michael, Steven and Ashley, for loving and supporting me during this rollercoaster ride called life. You all are my favorite and a treasured gift. I also want to thank my daughters-in-love, Stephanie and Samantha, for the special blessing they are to me.

CONTENTS

PREFACE

"I don't hear any India for you!" Yep, that was the first statement out of my mouth when my husband, Mike, came home from an India missions meeting held at our church. I just blurted it out! He told me that he felt like he was supposed to go to India on a missions' trip. What was this husband of mine thinking? Had he lost his mind? I was just starting to settle into my "new normal" and Mike sprung this bombshell on me. It had only been about a year and a half since my world got totally turned upside down -- for the better -- and now he wanted to mess that all up? I could feel the fear and uneasiness of my turbulent past start to creep back into my comfortable, safe world.

Did you ever have a set plan for your life that looked one way but took a drastic, unexpected turn in the opposite direction? A direction so foreign that it would take your breath away like you were punched hard in the stomach? A road that would leave you crying in despair? A direction that would fill you with loneliness, anxiety and fear? A dark place with no end in sight? A place filled with shame and disappointment? I'm sure you've been there before, even if you're not currently navigating that path.

See what God can do with an ordinary, stay-at-home mom and a self-employed electrician stuck in the cycle of addiction, shame and fear. He can do the same with you. I hope this book will challenge you and open your heart to pursue the great adventures the Lord has for your life.

1

Lots of Questions With No Answers

I t was the year 1979. I was 16 years old and had no more orthodontic appointments ahead of me with my braces finally off! A crazy summer of boy chasing had ended, school had started back and I was ready for my next adventure. I was always looking for fun and a laugh. It was September, the beginning my junior year at an all-girls, Catholic high school. The opportunity for me to meet some new boys was somewhat of a challenge, since my classmates were all the same sex. My circle of friends was small and the chances of finding a date, slim. It would be this year that my life would take a major turn.

High school was filled with laughter, goofing around, field hockey and dreams of being free from school. I liked to learn, for the most part, but I didn't want to do the homework. Did I really need to learn algebra? *Really?* Spanish? I don't even know anyone who speaks Spanish except my Spanish teacher. Even so, I can hardly understand her when she speaks English!

My future plans were to get married someday and have kids. Yep, have a husband, a family, buy a house, and live a quiet life. The white-picket-fence dream was just fine for me.

I could not see myself in college with books and studying. I wasn't applying myself in high school and I knew deep down that college wouldn't be any different for me. I liked to listen to music and get lost in it for hours. Headphones could drown out life's responsibilities with every rock song proclaiming lyrics I couldn't even decipher. I would even sleep with them on all night. I'm not talking about the little ear buds we see today. No, these were the big, bulky, full-sized ones that would silence any outside noise, yet do some major damage to your eardrums. Sorry to say, I'm sure that has affected my hearing, even to this day. Like I said, I just wanted to have fun.

School was not my thing except for the socializing part. Although, there was one particular class that I did truly love. Can you believe it was Theology? I loved learning about the stories in the Bible and this mysterious God that seemed so far away. I was raised Catholic, so belief in a higher being was not foreign to me. My parents loved God and attending church was non-negotiable. Every Sunday, off to church; or at least Saturday night Mass if we had plans on Sunday. My mom would tell us that Dad even made her go to church while they were on their honeymoon in Miami. It didn't matter if we were up the Pocono Mountains or down the Jersey shore on summer vacation; we went to church. Our family would vacation with three other families and I can still hear them mocking us as we left for Mass. I can remember Christmas morning, belly-aching about having to leave all my presents to go to church. My dad would remind us of how fortunate we were and that we could at least give God an hour a week in return. I mean, come on. One hour out of a whole week for having a roof over our heads, food on the table, good health and a happy family not marred with divorce? I secretly felt the same way deep down in my heart, but that didn't make church any less boring. I wasn't interested in the sermons and spent most of the time counting how many people wore glasses or scoping out the place for cute guys. Mass was so robotic; stand up, sit down, now kneel and stand back up. It wasn't too hard to zone out repeating the same prayers week after week. Every once in a while I would hear a sermon that pulled on my heart strings, but it was not the usual. Outside of church, I also kind of felt sorry for all the people that weren't Catholic because they were going to hell. That's what I was taught, anyway. But not me! Yes, I told lies, said the Lord's name in vain, smoked cigarettes and drank some beer, but we went to confession and wiped the slate clean. I remember thinking that if we got into a car accident on the way home from confession, zap! Right into Heaven we would go! Perfect and sinless, not having the chance to smudge that freshly cleaned record.

I also remember going to church with my grandparents when I was younger. They loved God, too. I will never forget my grandfather on his knees, praying and crying, missing my grandmother after she had passed away. So prayer was not an unusual thing in my family. The typical grace prayer at dinner time was a normal occurrence. I witnessed my parents praying. We prayed on our knees every Good Friday. We would pray the rosary as a family starting at 12 noon when Jesus was to have been hanging on the cross. The house would remain quiet until 3:00pm. How could you possibly listen to rock music or watch TV during that solemn time? It always seemed to get dark during that time of the day, too, which would make me feel like the crucifixion was really happening all over again. I would even recite my litany of prayers in the morning before jumping in the shower to start my day. I believed in the power of prayer, along with trying to earn my passage to Heaven. I had faith, but in what? That was one of many questions.

Oh, how I remember conversations with others about how great it would have been to have lived in the time of Adam and Eve, or even Moses. I pictured God talking to all His favorite people. How jealous I was to not be able to hear God talk to me personally. Why was He so silent? Images from the movie *The Ten Commandments* would swirl through my head as God would speak to Moses with that deep, powerful voice. I don't think I would have been brave enough to respond to a bush on fire with a deep, scary voice coming out of it. I probably would have been running down that mountain or shaking in my shoes like the cowardly lion from *The Wizard of Oz*! Oh, and the angel of death coming down from the sky as a green fog. Yikes! I think I was on my best behavior for a couple of days after watching that part. Anyway, that movie was my Bible, my measurement of the truth about God. I didn't think for one second that it couldn't be accurate. No way could someone make a movie about God and the Bible that would not be true, because God would strike them down dead, right? With the little bit of knowledge of the Bible that I did have, everything seemed to line up. That's just how it works...a little bit of truth and a little deception. Just enough to get you ensnared into a lie. How do you know when you're deceived? You don't. So I was very comfortable living in this delusional state with no one to challenge me or teach me.

That same year, my uncle had just purchased a house within walking distance and our family would go over to help out with renovations. As I entered my uncle's house, I saw a tan, muscular guy standing on a ladder. My attention was piqued as I noticed his full tool pouch hanging around his thin waist as he worked on overhead wires. It was lust at first sight! Yep, the hormones were in full gear. After a brief introduction, there was the typical small talk, but it didn't really matter what he said. He was tall with well-defined arms, and had these beautiful hazel eyes that could look right through me. Where did this hunk of flesh come from? My uncle was engaged to be married and this cute guy was his fiancé's baby brother. He was a "baby", all right. Mike worked as an electrician and drove a brand new, cherry red, Chevy Luv pickup truck. He was a nineteen-year-old guy with a real job and a nice vehicle. I was impressed!

Mike and I dated for five years. It was a volatile relationship, up and down, like a yo-yo. No wonder I had somewhat of a prayer life. Mike had a big chip on his shoulder, but he had a heart like I had never seen. He genuinely cared about his family and friends. Mike was a hard worker, extremely neat and a real go-getter. He was loyal to a fault and had a core group of friends that made the Three Stooges look like geniuses. If there was trouble, they would find it, or they would create some for themselves. These "friends" would also take advantage of his kindness and his wallet when it was time to buy the beer. They were fun, too, but had no sense of responsibility. Boy, opposites definitely do attract. These guys were all tatted up and had earrings way before it became somewhat popular, as it is today. My poor parents. It's a wonder they let me out of the house! God most certainly had His hand of protection upon me during that "know-it-all" teenage time. It would be a few short years later that those toxic relationships would end. Thank the Lord most of us do grow up and mature past the rebellion and lawlessness with some hard lessons well learned.

Mike and I continued to date and got engaged on Christmas Eve, 1982. We were opening presents at his mom's house before dinner. Mike had hidden the engagement ring in a pair of gloves, hoping I would slip it right on as I tested the fit. Unfortunately, the gloves were one size fits all, so I didn't bother to try them on until Mike insisted. I only tried on the right hand, thinking that would satisfy his futile request. It was comical as others tried to coax me into putting on the left hand glove while I insisted that if the right hand fit, then so would the left! Even then, my long fingernail had pushed the ring further up the glove when I placed it on. It wasn't until some odd questioning about what I felt in the left glove that I realized what was going on. We all laughed about me botching up his clever plot. Laughter was and still is a huge part of our relationship. I appreciated Mike's attempt to make the memorable event a special surprise for me.

Later that night, when I arrived home, I showed my parents the ring. They were very stoic in their response as I nervously told them our plans to marry a year and a half later. Mike had never asked my father for my hand in marriage. I don't know if it was because of his lack of training and not having a father involved in his life, or rebellion against my parents. I didn't ask about it, either. Being the first-born and only girl, I didn't have a sibling to follow and I became the trailblazer for my younger brothers. I'm sure it was extremely hurtful to them, although we never talked about it. Having a daughter gives me a whole new perspective and we certainly would be crushed if that honor was taken away from us. This omission was one of our many regrets.

The wedding planning was not like most. Things were difficult because Mike's parents had divorced when he was three.

There were many hurtful events that caused a lot of drama and people getting offended. We did finally marry on May 19, 1984 with a beautiful Catholic church ceremony followed by the typical Italian reception with all the trimmings. I still chuckle when I recall the caterer carving the flaming prime rib to the tune of Disco Inferno by The Trammps. Remember, this was 1984! Oh, and it didn't end there. We had a huge wedding cake with a water fountain in the center. The alcohol was flowing, as well as tears from the guests, as my grandfather serenaded me with a special song in between his own tears. My parents did their best to make what was a difficult day for them a beautiful day for me. They recognized early in the courtship that I was headed for trouble, yet they knew they couldn't stop it. Even the weather was prophetic as the day started out dark, gloomy and rainy, but later turned to clear, bright sunshine before all the festivities began. So I took the vows, for better or worse.

We went to Jamaica on our honeymoon and we were so naive of the real world. It was our first trip out of the country and now, as man and wife, we felt we could conquer the world. Sure, we could! We were so ignorant and I just remember all the warnings from the nationals about buying or selling drugs and getting locked up forever. I was so scared and I wasn't even a drug user! The Jamaicans drove us tourists past drug smuggling planes that had crashed and were left there rotting away as a reminder to others who may have the same idea. Yep, fear was the motivator for doing the right thing. I guess I brought that mentality home with me.

Our married life started out like our dating relationship -- fighting. Our fighting and yelling was our method of communicating and getting control. It would take twenty-some years later to begin to change it. We both had full-time jobs and after nine months of apartment dwelling, we bought our first house. My father was instrumental in scanning the newspapers for open houses and calling us up to go check them out. He gave us the confidence we needed to take a big financial step and buy. My dad had our back, just like our Heavenly Father has our back. We can accomplish so much more when we are not alone. So, at twenty-one and twenty-four, we were official homeowners. The house had great bones, but needed a lot of cosmetic work. All I can remember is that if you came to visit, you were handed a scraping tool to remove wallpaper. There was stubborn, hard to remove, dreadful wallpaper everywhere.

I had nightmares for months of removing wallpaper. It might look pretty on the one side, but what is it covering? I felt like the house. Things were looking good on the outside, but were a huge mess on the inside. Since we had spent all our money purchasing our home, things could get a little stressful. We worked long and hard hours, which is not a good mix with tension and horrible conflict resolution skills. Yet, we somehow managed to keep the marriage going forward. I liked getting dressed up, going out to lunch every day and talking with my girlfriends. My job required speaking with managers across the country. I liked chatting with them about their different cities, seasons and time zones. Boy, was it a setup for future events in my life.

After a few years, my girlfriend referred me for another job in the city. That was exciting for me, because the company was one of the giants in the state and we were in the heart of the bustling city. It was more fun, in my eyes, as now I could walk to places at lunchtime. The job also gave me the opportunity to travel to Philadelphia and work with some amazing people. My office had become a close-knit family and my boss was one of the nicest people I had ever met. He was an African American with the sweetest spirit. Growing up with racism all around, my compassion for others was nonexistent until Mr. Clark told me a story that had happened over a particular weekend. He had a prestigious job in our department with an excellent salary and his BMW model car reflected his success. While traveling on the interstate highway in his expensive luxury sedan doing the speed limit, he was pulled over because of his skin color. I could see the pain in his eyes as he retold the story to me. I think that this was the first time I really felt the sting of injustice. My heartstrings were being pulled and compassion for others of color began to grow in me.

I stayed at that job only a short time because, unexpectedly, I was being promoted to motherhood. I was sad leaving my professional family, but so excited to begin my own flesh and blood family. I had this complete fantasy picture in my head that every day would now be Saturday! I imagined leisurely waking up and not having to hurry out the door to fight the morning rush hour traffic. I visualized casually going about my day, snuggling and cuddling my sweet baby with no deadlines or bosses asking for reports or ringing phones to answer. Oh, what a lie. After Michael's birth, every day became Monday. There was no time off to just focus on me or paid vacation to go on expensive trips. Long gone were the lazy Saturdays where I could sleep in until noon if I felt like it. I was up even earlier than before, when I worked. Motherhood had me multitasking baths, bottles and baby. I now had a boss baby and yet, I was so happy to be a mom. I loved being the caretaker of my precious child and watching him grow, becoming more aware of this vast world. I thanked God daily that I was blessed to stay home and know my baby was getting my full attention. Yet, something was still off-kilter.

Our marriage was not getting better, as I thought it would with this sweet, new addition to our home. We were still fighting and focusing on each other's faults while trying desperately to fill the emptiness in our souls. We had legitimate needs for love, security and affirmation that were being met all the wrong ways. We were experts at playing the blame game and not having proper boundaries in our marriage. There were many outside voices causing division and resentment between us. Unrealistic expectations and criticism of each other became our norm. Each little dig was burying our marriage deeper and deeper into dispair. It was a recipe for disappointment and disaster.

 Father, where am I searching in the wrong place for the wrong things? I give You permission to reveal the areas where I have misplaced my affections, in Jesus' name.

2

Divine Encounter

A couple of years had passed and I had fought my last fight without seeing any hope of change with the way things were in my marriage. We were two unhappy and unfulfilled people, desperate for relief. We were looking for something more that would make this life worth living and bring peace to our souls. We had a one-and-a-half-year-old son, Michael, who brought much joy into the home. He was a great baby and an awesome toddler. The love we had for this child was powerful, yet Mike used alcohol to fill his void and I depended on people-pleasing to fill mine. Did it work? Of course not! I knew something or someone needed to change, and it wasn't me.

Then on Friday, December 7th, 1990, I was done. I needed to get out of this toxic relationship and Mike needed to quit drinking and get ahold of his emotions. This was my solution to this never-ending merry-go-round that was not so merry. After Mike had left for work following another major fight, I called my dad explaining that I wanted to move back home. My parents had witnessed some of the tension in the marriage, so my decision was not totally unexpected. Dad quickly drove over to my house, silently dismantled the baby's crib while I packed my clothes, and we left. Feelings of defeat, failure, and shame, and yet a quiet calm filled my soul. I was so angry that it had reached this point, but I also felt bad that this was the way Mike dealt with pain. It would be years later before I would truly understand the depths of that pain, and my own dysfunction as well.

My father had arranged a meeting with a lawyer that same day to discuss my options. He also described in detail, step-by-step how Mike would respond to my sudden departure. What a blessing that meeting was, so that I would have advanced knowledge of the explosion to come and that it would be typical behavior for our situation. Hours later, when Mike arrived home from work, the anticipated eruption of anger occurred when he realized I was gone. We didn't have cell phones, texting or social media back then, but my parents only lived a mile away, so he knew where to find me. What clothes I had left behind were now dumped on the driveway, as the lawyer had predicted. The heat on the stove was being turned up, but I now no longer felt that I would be burned. I would learn that God had a mighty plan.

Once the anger subsided, which took a couple of days, Mike agreed to go to marriage counseling. We never wanted to divorce and it's true that hurt people, hurt people. Mike's childhood was scarred from divorce and we certainly didn't want to continue the curse into our own family. We just didn't know how to make things better without assistance. I was determined not to move back home until we both could have better communication skills. I started investigating all sorts of support groups from Al-Anon to Emotions Anonymous. They helped me somewhat, but I really felt like something was missing. We were able to find a marriage counselor that we both liked through Catholic Charities. He provided us with some much needed conflict resolution techniques, along with a place to talk about our issues. Hope was rising as I started to see some positive results within our marriage. Still, I felt something was lacking.

In the meantime, my mom had a membership to a fitness club around the corner. She came home from the club weeks later to tell me that she had met a woman who counseled women in bad relationships for free. Really? That sounded wonderful, being a stay-at-home mom with no extra income. The only requirement was that I had to make the initial contact. Not a problem! I dialed the phone and set up the first appointment. February 5th, 1991 was the beginning of discovering what was missing. Walking in, I was feeling so low and broken, yet felt love and compassion from a complete stranger. Vivian was a beautiful woman in her early forties with a confidence and strength that made me feel safe and secure. As I was warmly welcomed in, she shared some of her personal story with me and gave me some insight as to my situation as well. I was in the right place. Vivian also mentioned a women's Bible study that she taught in her home. She encouraged me to come, but what could I learn? I had four years of theology classes in high school and I prayed every day. I just wanted this marriage (husband) fixed and a happy, quiet life. I was not interested in a group where I could possibly be more exposed for making a bad choice for a marriage partner or become some holy roller.

As the weeks passed by, I became stronger and more confident in myself as I continued attending Al-Anon and Emotions Anonymous meetings. I saw people that were there for years and still seemed kind of hopeless in my eyes. I think those meetings were a good start for me, but I felt it was a temporary stop. I did not want to live the rest of my life attending meetings rehashing the same issues. I needed freedom, and something was tugging at my heart. I eventually moved back home with Mike, since our relationship seemed to be on the mend. We were committed to couple's counseling and I also continued my counseling with Vivian. I was intrigued how she had Scripture to meet my every need. She had such a peace about her and a confidence for which I longed. Finally, after about a year, she asked me that if I died, where did I think I would go? "Heaven, of course!" I responded so arrogantly.

"Why?" she continued to gently prod.

"Because I'm a good person!" I answered her, getting a little annoyed. It's not like she didn't know me. She heard my story of the nice, Catholic girl marrying the jerk! Did she not get it? Was she blind to all I endured to keep this marriage together?

How do you know when you are deceived? You don't. As she continued to explain that the Bible states that none are good and we cannot earn our way to Heaven, her words were bringing life and shedding light into my dark heart of pride and self-righteousness. All of a sudden, I didn't feel so confident. The Word of God is living and powerful, sharper than a two-edged sword, and I was getting pierced directly in my heart. Truth was exposing the curtain of lies that had enshrouded me. Jesus was cutting away deception and darkness with each Scripture I heard.

Vivian asked me if I wanted to repeat the sinner's prayer to truly invite Jesus into my life. As I did, I felt a weight being lifted off of me. I had not recognized the oppression before, but I surely felt it lift. A new joy filled my spirit. I finally felt alive. I understood why Jesus said that we needed to be born again. I had a new birthdate and my name was officially recorded in the Lamb's book of life. Now, I wanted to go to the Bible study in a curious kind of way. I wanted to learn about what God had to say instead of man's great ideas that left me empty and confused. Who is this great God that put up with such nonsense for so long? Who is this God that was chasing me down, causing this deep thirst for more? What was sustaining me?

It was not *what*, but *Who* was sustaining me, and His name was Jesus. I could not get enough of Bible study. I would sit and ponder through the prayer and Scripture teaching. I felt like the wheels in my head were spinning as I tried to filter through what I had been taught in religious education classes versus the Truth. A renewing of my mind was taking place. When all the other women had gone home, I would pick Vivian's brain for hours. Sometimes it would be one o'clock in the morning as I drove home. Not a big deal for a young teenager, but I was a busy mom with two young kids now, and this was a school night! I would pray for divine strength to get me up in a few hours and be functional. I thank God for the personal time Vivian poured into me. It was a huge sacrifice for not only her, but her husband, too. I would show up week after week with my list of questions that would come up after searching the Scriptures. I would listen like the Ethiopian eunuch in Acts chapter 8 who had Phillip explain to him the meaning of the Word. I was like a sponge, absorbing every drop, only to be later squeezed out to others. That's exactly what God did.

I had a neighbor who lived two houses away. We both had small boys, born months apart. It could be lonely at times as a stay-at-home mom with a child that wanted all my attention. I missed real adult communication and interaction from my previous, corporate world. I had a husband who worked hard and provided a beautiful home for his family. Unfortunately, though, I was trying to meet his needs with the love language that was needed to fulfill mine. He needed my respect and acts of service. I needed to share all that I was learning in my new relationship with Jesus. Mike's drinking increased along with his frustration towards my spiritual awakening. He wasn't interested in God and mocked anything that had to do with the Bible. He thought he was pretty clever combining the names Mother Teresa and Lisa forming "Sister Tralisa" as his new condescending nickname for me. Yet, I marveled how he never stopped me from attending any event or Bible study.

So, my neighbor Karen and I became instant friends as our kids played together. We had many common interests; heavy chain smoking, painting our long fingernails, drinking frozen drinks and playing double solitaire. We could talk about husband issues and play a mean game of cards for hours! It was an outlet to express my feelings to another that was facing some similar problems, as well. It is so important to have a safe place to share your heart, a secure place where you are not judged or condemned. We came from the same Catholic background, so I was excited to share with her all I was learning about God. She was not able to come with me to the Bible study at night because of her husband's second shift work schedule. I would go on Thursday night to Vivian's, and then regurgitate the entire lesson the following night with her. So Friday night after the children were put to bed, Mike would stay home watching TV and drinking beer, and I would go to Karen's house. We would drink our favorite frozen cocktail, smoke cigarettes and have Bible study. We would still manage a game or two of cards so I could beat her! Boy, God will use any opportunity if we let Him. Not that I recommend our unhealthy behavior. We both eventually quit smoking, but lung cancer would later claim the life of this dear friend many years later.

My point is that God will meet us where we are when we seek Him. He didn't force me to clean up; I chose to with only His grace and mercy! It was His divine grace, not the sloppy grace that excuses our bad behavior and choices. No, I'm referring to His grace that leads me to look and act more like Jesus. His Word promises that if we draw near to Him, He will draw near to us. Well, He certainly fulfilled His Word. Now with Karen seeking and learning about God, my list of questions doubled and so did my time searching the Scriptures! How awesome to seek the Lord for answers and He responds. I could not get enough of this new relationship with the God of the Universe and now my personal God.

I was finally experiencing my Heavenly Father and His unfailing love for me. The words were coming alive off the page and my love for others was expanding. Things became much clearer. My thoughts towards my husband became more positive and forgiving. I was learning to get my affirmation and purpose from God, not people. Did I become an upstanding, perfect Christian? No. The walk with Christ is a process, and mine had begun. Did my circumstances change? Yes. For the better? No. Mike and I would go through cycles of really, really good or really, really bad. What did change was my heart and my understanding that God does talk to us today!

I did have unshakeable peace when I read my Bible. My mind was being renewed and a deep relationship with Jesus was developing. As I learned more of who God was, I was learning more of who I was. My outside circumstances were no longer dictating my emotions or decisions. I was fixed and focused on Jesus and His perfect plans for me. I had resolved myself to stay the course. I held onto the scripture, "For the Lord God will help me; Therefore, I will not be disgraced; Therefore, I have set My face like flint, and I know that I will not be ashamed," (Isaiah 50:7). God's promises were more real to me than anything I could tangibly see or feel. Faith was rising in greater and greater measures. The invisible God was becoming visible to me in my circumstances, and what a sight to behold!

 Father, please shine Your light and open my eyes in the areas that I don't know You, in Jesus' name.

3

Husband To The Husbandless

It was a brisk day in October 1996 and my heart was hurting. My niece that I had babysat for a year and a half was gone. My brother had been transferred down to North Carolina and I was mourning this child. This toddler had become the little girl we didn't have in our male dominant family. I was so excited when my sister-in-law asked if I would watch Amanda a couple days a week. I was already in Heaven staying home with my own second son, Steven, who was seventeen months older. He was the sweetest little guy with a huge heart. Adding a newborn to the mix thrilled the both of us. The joy turned to a deep sadness when they moved south. I was trying to get into a new routine now and wanted to take advantage of the weather before winter arrived. So I bundled up my Steven and strapped him into the baby seat on the back of my bike and off we went. It was a beautiful autumn day with bright sunshine warming my face as we biked around the neighborhood. I wanted to go to the park where I would normally take the kids in the stroller to look at the fish in the creek that separated the neighborhoods. It was a small, wooded area that had a steel bridge that crossed over a narrow stream. Local teenagers liked to hang out there to smoke and drink, since there were many areas to conceal illegal behavior. The little kids liked it, too, because we were able to spot various wildlife, depending on the season. Well, this day would prove to be one I will never forget.

As I pedaled across the small bridge, my left hand and handlebar hit the metal railing, causing some mild pain. When I looked down at my hand, I heard a *ping* as I saw the empty prongs from my engagement ring piercing through my cotton glove. I felt all the blood in my head drain to my feet as panic and fear tried to overtake me. Immediately, I surmised that the diamond was jolted out of the setting, hit the bridge (which was the *ping* sound I heard), and fell through the grates. Nervously, I parked the bike and whisked my toddler out of his seat. He was a bit confused as to why our excursion had halted so abruptly. I frantically explained to him that the diamond had fallen out of my ring and I needed to find it. He so innocently asked what the diamond looked like and I told him it was shiny. He said, "Don't worry, Mommy. I'll find it." Of course, I really didn't expect a three-year-old to find it, yet his confidence was somewhat comforting.

I just needed him out of the way while I prayed and searched through the gravel and mud. It was cute when Steven held up a shiny, aluminum beer can tab and asked if that was it. I mean, it did qualify as "shiny" in the eyes of a young child, but the cuteness wore off quickly as the pit in my stomach deepened and still no diamond. *Really God?! This is the last thing I need right now. It's not bad enough that my heart is shredded from losing my niece, but now my diamond, too?*

Reluctantly, I went back home to call my dad with the hopes that he would be around to help me and somehow make this nightmare evaporate. After I dialed the phone, I only heard his recorded voice on the answering machine. Again, the fear tried to paralyze me with thoughts of never having a wedding ring. My engagement ring and wedding band were custom made to fit into each other, so the wedding band could not be worn alone. I certainly could not wear my engagement ring with empty prongs scratching and poking everything I touched. Then the horrible thoughts of Mike's reaction played through my mind. I just imagined a rage of anger as he would scream about how expensive it would be to replace it and how we didn't have it in our budget. Thoughts of some neighborhood kid finding it or disturbing the site so that the diamond would be lost forever flashed through my head. It was a real battle to silence those voices and just pray for God's peace. I remembered the Scripture that He keeps those in perfect peace whose mind is stayed on Him because he trusts in Him (Isaiah 26:3). So that's what I did. I couldn't change what happened, but I could focus on the One who loves me and cares about me.

Later that day, I noticed my girlfriend was home from her college class. Lauren lived across the street with her parents. She was a born again believer, too, and we would spend hours talking about the goodness of the Lord. I just felt that she would be able to at least pray for me, so I ran over to her house and knocked on the door. When I had explained what happened, her unshakable faith arose and she declared that together we would find the diamond. I felt a little flicker of hope arise in me. Lauren grabbed some latex gloves and a bucket, since we would be down by the creek and it was not the cleanest place. As we walked back to the location, we

21

prayed out loud scriptures about God's goodness and faithfulness to His kids. My faith was soaring by the time we reached the dreaded spot. Lauren went to work immediately, sifting through the yuck. I just stood on the bank, praying silently. I told the Lord that I surrendered the diamond to Him and I trusted Him whether I would somehow find it now or it would get replaced later. However, I did mention to God how special that particular stone was to me because Mike had personally picked it out, along with the unique setting. Even though currently the marriage was horrible, that diamond represented a time when the relationship was filled with so much hope and promise for the future.

I heard God speak ever so gently to my heart. He asked, "Who made that diamond?"

I answered immediately. "Well, You, Lord. This diamond was not man-made and probably took many years to form."

The conversation continued as He asked, "What was it made to do?"

I responded, "It's made to reflect light." At that very moment, a bright beam of light shot up from the ground and hit me directly in the eyes. I bent down and picked up my diamond. I raised my hand up to Heaven, clutching the stone tightly between my thumb and finger and said, "Thank you!"

Lauren and I just witnessed a miracle! We were in awe, jumping for joy, knowing that the God of the Universe, our Father had not only heard the cry of my heart, but answered! It was such a divine encounter with God's divine timing. The sun was not in position in the sky to reflect off that stone until that exact time when I could be there. His perfect timing! My hands were shaking and tears were streaming down my face as we rushed back home to share the supernatural occurrence.

I had the diamond re-set with extra prongs for added security. As I look back and ponder what the Lord did on that fall day, I am still in awe. As I look down at the stone on my finger, I'm reminded of the Israelites. God had commanded them in the wilderness to pick up stones and build an altar of remembrance. Why? So that every time they would pass by that location, they would remember how the Lord acted on their behalf. They would be reminded of His awesome love and faithfulness to His beloved. How fortunate I am to be able to wear my altar of remembrance on my hand daily! I don't need to travel by foot for days to another city or some wilderness to remember. To this day, when my faith is wavering, I look down at my stone and remember God's faithfulness to me. I remember that I serve a God of the impossible, a loving and intimate God who deeply cares about the things that are important to me. I remember a personal God who hears me and responds, not because of who I am but because of who He is. Do you have an altar of remembrance? I'm sure if you take the time to think back on some of the trials of your life and wonder how in the world you survived, you would see the hand of God, too.

The ring was repaired immediately, but it would take another eight years before the marriage would undergo the same "re-setting". As the diamond was knocked out of its four-prong setting adding to my pain and trauma, the Lord has used it for my good and the advancement of His kingdom. I had to release my precious diamond and say, "Not my will be done, but Yours." I believe it was the combination of releasing my will and my wants and joining my faith with another believer in my Heavenly Father that I had an immediate response from

God. I also acknowledge that it was God's gracious mercy and favor that covered me.

The other amazing fact about this story is how the Lord keeps giving me more insight about His extravagant love for me when I retell it to others. When I was preparing for a marriage seminar and reflecting (pardon the pun) on this particular miracle in my life that I wanted to share, again the Lord showed me that as I was in covenant with a man, my husband, I was also in covenant with my God. Yet, the covenant with God is so much greater. He is the One that was required to give all. His Son Jesus paid the price so that I could be in relationship with Father God for eternity and would never have to suffer separation. God is the one who pursues and provides for me, and my part is just to respond to His unfailing love. The Bible tells us that He first loved us (1 John 4:19). Unlike man, God will never leave me nor forsake me. What a comfort, knowing He is so faithful and keeps His Word. He is a covenant keeper. I never have to second guess His intentions towards me or worry about Him changing His mind. As Mike had given me an engagement ring, my God now had given me an engagement ring signifying our eternal covenant. He truly was and is a Husband to the husbandless. God is always demonstrating His fierce love for us, but we just don't recognize it.

Another lesson I learned is about that word many are not fond of: *time*. It takes a long time for high temperatures and high pressure on carbon to crystalize into diamonds. I was certainly feeling the heat and being squeezed by the pressure, but it wasn't until I found Jesus that I could endure those circumstances for years. It would take years for me to be changed so that I could begin to reflect the light of Christ to others. I don't become discouraged because it is an on-going process that won't be complete until that day I see Jesus face to face. As I look down at all the facets in the diamond, I think about all the different facets of God. I am to reflect all those elements to others who have never experienced Jesus. What an honor and a privilege to a lost and hurting world so desperate to know the truth.

 Father, help me to fully receive Your perfect love and reflect it to others, in Jesus' name.

4

Eggs Aren't What They Are Cracked Up To Be

In 2001, our daughter Ashley had made her entry into our family. She was a complete surprise to all of us. Initially, the boys were a bit disappointed with the news because we had moved past the kiddie stage for amusement rides and this would be a setback to vacation options. Michael was twelve and Steven was about to turn eight, so needless to say, all my baby paraphernalia was long gone. However, it wasn't long before excitement for this new little one grew. Everyone was guessing the sex and, because we already had two lovable boys, the anticipation was great. I often wondered if this baby was sent from above to help our hurting hearts after losing my dad two years prior to lung cancer.

We were still learning to navigate life without him. His diagnosis came as a complete shock. My dad was the picture of health, joyfully telling us he had the heart of a twenty-year-old. Those were the very words told to him by a medical professional months earlier, following a complete physical exam. My mom always feared he would have a heart attack, so now we could all relax, knowing that would not be the case. About a year later, Dad experienced tremendous pain in his rib cage after swinging a golf club. After some tests, the silent killer was revealed. I'll never forget the phone call with the devastating news of stage 4 cancer. Cancer in his lungs had metastasized, weakening his ribs and causing a break.

I reasoned in my mind that there had to be a mistake. His medical records must have gotten mixed up with someone else's. "Lord, not my dad," I softly whispered. He truly was a great father figure who was adored by many. I couldn't tell you how many different prayer lists from all over included his name. Unfortunately, Dad's strong heart was no match for the cancer, and he was gone in nine months. We all felt the blow of his premature death at age sixty-two. His love and trust in the Lord gave me great comfort, knowing I would see him again in Heaven. I also thought about him seeing this child before any of us on this side of eternity.

My sister-in-law was also pregnant with her second child, and the due dates weren't that far apart. She delivered her daughter, Melissa, first. Ten days later, Ashley was actually born on her due date, and we cheered wildly as the doctor announced we had a girl! Life seemed wonderful. The boys loved their little sister like nothing I had ever seen. They fought over who would push the stroller and who was loved more by Ashley. I sometimes had to remind them that I was the mother and I needed time with her, as well. This child was also an unspoken answered prayer for Mike. He certainly loved his boys and was so proud of them, but he yearned for a little girl. His heart strings were pulled from day one.

Despite the joy of this answered prayer, Mike and I noticed a shift in our oldest son as he entered into his teen years. He was more distant, school was a huge challenge and conflict was the norm. Grounding seemed to be the punishment of choice, since this was well before kids had cell phones. We figured he must really want to hang with us parents, because his choices were not changing. It was an extremely difficult time for all of us.

The year 2004 was the craziest year for us. In May, Mike and I celebrated our twentieth wedding anniversary in Cancun, Mexico. We had *never* gone away alone as a couple after having kids. It's not that we didn't have a babysitter or the time to get away. We didn't realize the huge benefit of investing in just *us* and not always putting the kids first. This is one mistake I would not repeat if you want a successful marriage. It is healthy for you and your spouse, as well as for the children, to have some time apart. I can't say it was easy pulling out of the driveway while the youngest (who was three at the time) cried. My heartstrings were being stretched further than ever before, but we all managed to survive.

During our second honeymoon, we enjoyed the freedom of being alone with no kid interference for several days, until a couple we met at the resort asked if we wanted to swap partners. Well, I should say the husband asked. We had met them earlier that evening after dinner. They were from Wales and spoke with the best accent. We exchanged the normal pleasantries and they seemed like a nice couple around our age. We were invited up to their hotel room as the lounge area was extremely noisy with music and conversation was difficult. I was always looking for an excuse to witness Jesus to others, and I wasn't going to let this opportunity get away.

As I was talking about the Bible and Jesus with the wife in their room, Mike and the husband were having a beer and talking outside on the balcony. The man proposed his "switchems" plan, and Mike blew up, asking him if he knew how to fly! That man almost got tossed off the seventh floor balcony after suggesting his perverted idea to Mike. The sliding glass door flung open and Mike stormed in, declaring that it was time for us to go, immediately. I was confused by the abrupt and seemingly rude exit, thinking it was another drunken outburst. When we returned to our hotel room, Mike explained the reason for his anger. I was proud of how my husband stood up to protect me, but felt bad for the other wife. If she was in on it, she surely didn't let on to me. I know that people do all kinds of crazy, sexually immoral things, but I had never personally been approached before. I thank God for His protection. Unfortunately, that was not what we had in mind in meeting new friends and, happily, we didn't see them the remainder of our getaway.

We really did receive so much favor during that trip that no one could deny the hand of God at work. Just to name one, we requested an upgrade for our room and were given one of the few penthouse rooms with a balcony. Others had many complaints about the resort, yet we were walking in blessings. God was working on Mike's heart continually. Here and there, I could see little glimpses of a softening and recognizing that this God really did exist. I believe the trip was a setup for what God was up to next.

In the fall of the same year, school had started back up and everyone was easing into their routine. The peace didn't last long, as our house became the target of vandalism with some troubled youth. Every Friday and Saturday night, our home would be pelted by eggs. Our boys would wake up to the terrifying sound of something hitting their bedroom windows. Oh, it became such a nightmare. The children were so scared. My husband and the oldest would sometimes fight because we felt that there was some type of connection with his so-called friends.

Week after week, this torture repeated itself; kids crying and me calling 911. The scripture that "He works all things together for good," (Romans 8:28) was a comfort to me, even though I had not yet witnessed the good. I would just pull out my Bible and start reading until the authorities arrived to fill out another police report. This time, I made an agreement with God. I told Him that I didn't care if the vandals climbed up on the roof and poured black paint all over the house; I just wanted our family saved. Whatever it took, I was ready for the battle. *Whatever it took*! I was ready for a move of God and didn't want to remain the same. It is a dangerous prayer to pray because, sometimes, it has to get even worse before it gets better, but I was done playing around and I meant business.

As I prayed about the traumatic situation, the Lord told me to start with the senior pastor of the church where Michael attended youth group. Yes, this Catholic teen was attending a non-denominational, charismatic Protestant youth group at church on Sunday nights with my girlfriend's son. The same girlfriend that I poured into eleven years previously. Karen had moved out of the Catholic Church and had been a member there for a couple of years. Her schedule had changed and she was now able to attend the Bible study with me. Ironically, the Bible study met at this same church for a season. Karen would take Michael with her to the church youth group. Michael seemed to enjoy his time there and I was happy for the positive influence. This group didn't have a permanent youth pastor at the time. There were parent leaders keeping the program afloat until the position could be filled permanently. Some of those leaders were in my Bible group.

Why did the Lord want me to start with the senior pastor? I had no clue. I had never met this man. I had heard he was a godly man with a kind heart, but he was a complete stranger to me and our family. I felt the Lord tell me to call and schedule an appointment with Pastor Bill. I shared this unusual prompting with Mike. He was so fed up with all the nonsense that he agreed to accompany me if I could get an appointment. Surprisingly, what I thought would be a battle seemed pretty effortless. Great!

Knowing what was at stake, I asked for prayer support from friends who were members of Immanuel Church. Some thought that the meeting would be difficult to schedule because the church secretary was very protective of the pastor. I nervously made the call and they were correct. She was not going to let just anyone waltz in and waste the pastor's time. He had his own congregation to attend to and their needs superseded any outsider's request. She made that fact perfectly clear to me as I requested an appointment. I was determined to follow through with what I believed the Lord had instructed me to do, and I was not backing down. After some explanation for the meeting, the date was set for Wednesday, October 27th, 2004. One victory accomplished!

Prayers continued up to the final, solemn steps into the pastor's private office. The room was warm and inviting, with a full bookcase lining the backwall behind his wood desk. Pastor Bill started with some pleasantries and the next thing I knew, he was speaking some of the exact things that I had privately said only to the Lord. Don't ever believe God doesn't hear or know your deepest heart cries. I felt great comfort as I felt the

Holy Spirit confirm to me His presence right there in that very moment. I remained silent as I watched Pastor Bill minister to a man full of childhood rejection, abandonment and pain that desperately wanted to help his own son. Pastor Bill began to speak things that pierced Mike's heart. Slowly, some bricks around Mike's heart were being loosened. He began to weep and confess the revelation that the Michael that needed help was not his son, but Mike himself. What a turning point!

Pastor Bill was hearing the Lord clearly and responding with such accuracy that Mike was able to receive ministry from him. The Father's heart of love, without judgment or condemnation, was being demonstrated by Pastor Bill. This was a foreign concept to Mike, since it was never modeled by his own father. The proverbial boat had left the dock and there was no turning back! Healing had begun and the Healer was continuing His mighty work. As we walked toward the door after our session ended, Pastor Bill casually mentioned possibly seeing us on Sunday. My heart was secretly jumping with excitement, yet I calmly watched as Mike answered with a coy, "Maybe."

I longed to go to a church that not only studied the Word of God, but was on fire for Jesus. I didn't mind going to the Catholic Mass because God met me right where I was. I could enter into His Presence and His peace would just envelope me like a warm, cozy blanket. I was thankful to be there, but I also felt that there was so much more. I yearned for true fellowship among people that wanted to worship God not out of religious duty, but pure devotion. I remember praying about my heart's desire for more and the Lord telling me that I needed to stay under my husband's covering, which meant I was to follow him. If he would go to the Catholic church, then that was where I needed to be. If the Lord wanted to move us to a different church, it would be through Mike. So I stayed put in the Catholic church out of obedience, and the Lord met me there every time.

It wasn't the same boring Mass and ritual from childhood. The hymns had special meaning and, now that the veil was removed from my eyes, they were declarations of God's faithfulness and goodness to me. Many times, I couldn't even get the words out as tears of gratefulness rolled down my cheeks. I was astonished that some of the songs were actual scripture. I even remember my mother telling me that one of our neighbors had commented to her about seeing the peace on my face during the service. Someday, I hope to be carrying the glory of God where I would need to wear a veil like Moses when he came down the mountain and it blinded people.

The ride home was amazing, as Mike could not understand how a man could spend so much time counseling with us and not expect or accept payment. Pastor Bill refused when Mike had offered to pay him for his services. In a world where money seems to be the main driving force, it was refreshing to witness the power of the love of God given so freely. Free for us, but we know the great price Jesus paid for that freedom; death on a cross.

Now the adventure began. We did attend the following Sunday service at Immanuel instead of our home church. Mike had felt something different when our family walked through the doors. There were greeters and people smiling that left us with a warm and welcoming spirit. When we dropped off three-year-old Ashley in the kids' church, everyone was so friendly and pleasant. Boy, are first impressions important! You just don't know who you may impact and these believers were a huge, positive influence. We could feel the love of Christ permeate through each one. As we entered the sanctuary, I was so excited as the service began. Yep, most of the congregation was singing and worshiping their King with not only their voices, but arms waving high. Their worship team was also a full band, with drums and all! My husband was accustomed to classical old hymns and only a pipe organ. I can't even imagine what he was thinking. Immanuel Church looked like a traditional Baptist church on the exterior with red brick, a tall steeple and beautiful windows, but was very much charismatic on the inside.

My friend Karen, who was a member of Immanuel, was a nervous wreck that day. She was very familiar with Mike's outbursts and distaste of the things of God. She knew Mike's tendencies and she was just waiting to see his impatience and anger kick in. Why? Well, as an ex-Catholic, and she was familiar with the time frame of most Sunday Masses. It wasn't unusual to be in and out of church, actually in your car, pulling out of the parking lot in forty-five minutes. Immanuel had already exceeded that with just their worship team!   Mike had never been exposed to this type of worship before and my friend knew it. Was this place going to push him over the limit? I thought, whether this was a one-time deal or not, I was going to enjoy every second. I was so absorbed in the freedom of expression to my Jesus, I did not even notice what Mike was doing. He told me later that he just stood there with arms folded, looking at all these crazy people. Worship ended and he hadn't gone storming out of the church in anger, yet.

While I was sitting in the pew, I opened the church bulletin and a sermon note-guide fell out. The note-guide was a tool Pastor Bill developed for the congregation to use at home for further study. It had scripture references and blank spaces to add your own notes. It was like a mini Bible study. I noticed that he was teaching in the middle of a sermon series. I wondered how this would work out since we had not been present for the previous teachings. Pastor Bill, being the great teacher that he was, had no problem going back and hitting the highlights from the former messages as a refresher, and then proceeding with the new lesson.

At the end of his sermon, he asked for a show of hands of the ones that did not know if they would go to Heaven if they died that night. Suddenly, Mike's arm shots up like a rocket and my jaw dropped like a fifty-pound weight! Yes, I had prayed for Mike. Yes, I wanted salvation for him. Yes, I wanted to share my walk with the Lord with Mike. Yes, I wanted him to be a great husband and father. But right now? It was his very first time in this church. I had no warning or sign from the heavens. I was in complete shock! Could this really be happening at this very moment? I was stunned as I watched Mike stand up and go forward for the altar call. It was like it was happening in slow motion. My mind could not comprehend what my eyes were seeing.

My friends were just as surprised as he stood straight up and walked past all these strangers to go to the front of the sanctuary. God really has a sense of humor, because all these inner city kids followed Mike up as well. A young woman had brought them to church that day and when the altar call was made, they responded, too. Mike looked like the Pied Piper with all these children following him. What made it so funny to me was that Mike was extremely prejudiced at that time, and here he was, surrounded by a whole group of African American kids. As he recited the sinner's prayer and accepted Jesus into his heart, life as I knew it would never be the same! The years of generational hate and prejudice would be replaced with love and deep, lasting relationships with all ethnicities.

What was so interesting as well was the date. It was October 31st, Halloween, the day of the year I hated the most. Why? I just had a strong conviction not to participate in the celebration of evil. I don't believe it is evil to wear a costume, or knock on a neighbor's door and eat candy. Everything from the decorations to the meaning behind Halloween rituals glorify fear and death. It's Satan's high holy day and I prefer to not have any part in it. I found healthier alternatives for my children that were not celebrating darkness and they would have fun and fellowship, along with piles of candy. The day I dreaded the most was now one of my favorites. Our household would forever be turned upside down that day and set on a new course as the ship left the harbor!

 Father, give me courage to stay on the path that is in opposition to the world, in Jesus' name.

5

The Day After

After Mike gave his heart to the Lord, things started to change. It was a slow change, but it was a change. He started reading books. Of course he read the newspaper, mostly the sports page, but I'm talking about real books now. The books with a thick, hard cover that had some weight to them, both physically and intellectually. He would devour them! We actually had to buy a bookcase to hold them all. He also started listening to worship music. It seemed like every night for a couple of months straight, it was the same routine. After dinner, the music would be turned on while he laid on the family room floor, reading his Bible and crying. Michael W. Smith's Worship CD was his favorite. The Lord would just minister to him through that music night after night. As the tears flowed, his heart was being massaged and softened. The Bible also came alive as the Lord directed him to read certain scriptures. Yes, he was being directed not by an audible voice, but by an impression in his spirit. The insight he would receive was amazing. He was also able to quote scripture. This may not seem so spectacular, but he was also able to give the chapter and verse! I know that was *only* God. Yes, Mike was always good with numbers, but this was way too much. We were seeing the hand of God move mightily!

I always wondered how God would work it out so that Mike could truly be the spiritual head of the house. I had spent all those years in Bible study and the only Bible Mike ever opened was the one he would throw across the room in anger, so that it landed on the floor and popped open. How would he ever catch up to be the man God called him to be? How was he going to get thirteen years of Bible study under his belt to be able to lead our family?

Ha! Nothing is impossible with God, and He continued to demonstrate His great power to us in supernatural ways. Mike suffered for forty years from debilitating back pain. It was discovered as a young child that he had an abnormal narrowing of his lower spine. He had spent countless weeks in traction at the Nemours Children's Hospital with no relief. Medicating his pain with alcohol and prescription drugs as a teenager was his answer. Ultimately, scar tissue accumulated as a result of back surgery at thirty-six for a bulging disc and added to the hopelessness of a life sentence of physical pain. It was frustrating for me and I felt completely helpless as I watched Mike, day after day, crawl to the shower to alleviate the excruciating pain. With tears in his eyes, we prayed, believing this was not God's will for Mike. We renounced and broke agreement with all words spoken that were in opposition to the Word of God. The next morning, Mike woke up completely pain free! He was healed! We praised the Lord for a miraculous answer to a forty-year battle of affliction. Mike's bondage to alcoholism and a prescription drug addiction were miraculously healed, as well, months later. We were witnessing the scripture John 8:31-32,

"If you abide in My word, you are My disciples indeed. And you shall know the truth, and the truth shall make you free."

The vast cavern between the two of us was narrowing and our conversations expanding. I finally had a life partner with whom I could discuss, at length, the deep things of God. I have to honestly admit that, as happy as I was to see the change and anointing on Mike, I was a little jealous. With all my study of Scripture, it came so much easier for him. The jealousy didn't last long, as we would marvel at His goodness towards us. What a joy to share the longings of our hearts together! I believe we were finally connecting the way God intended a husband and wife to relate to each other. God was showing us the true picture of marriage. It was no longer one-sided, but a partnership with the Maker of marriage. With God at the center of our relationship, everything else was improving.

Did we stop annoying each other? No. There were times when I was tired and just wanted to sleep, but Mike would want to share about God. He would keep talking into the late hours of the night while I struggled to stay awake, wishing he would just wait and tell me in the morning. There were other times when the Holy Spirit would start us laughing; not just a little chuckle but the loud, uncontrollable belly laughs. I'm sure the kids didn't appreciate it, especially since they weren't in on the joke. Did we stop fighting? No. We would just apologize and forgive more quickly, most of the time. We were not only learning tools to keep us from killing each other but most importantly, our hearts were softening. We were learning to appreciate our differences and giftings, seeing each other through the eyes of Christ instead of our self-serving view. Mike was also being mentored by Pastor Bill, who provided much wisdom and inner healing, and a strong friendship developed between them.

Our prayer life changed, as well. Actually, my prayer life changed and Mike began one. I noticed someone missing in the early hours of the morning from our bed. Mike would be up before dawn, alone downstairs, in the family room praying. I loved to sleep and I loved God, but I wasn't leaving my nice warm spot when it was still dark outside. Faithfully, every morning Mike was up. I kind of felt guilty staying in my cozy cocoon, but why couldn't we just pray together later? I needed my sleep and besides, I had prayed for years by myself. Now it was his turn as the head of the house, at least that's how I would justify my selfish position.

Soon, I felt a tugging on my heart again to get up and join my husband. I have to confess that the thought of a nice, hot cup of coffee helped motivate me, too. I would put a fresh pot on as soon as I reached the kitchen and wait for it to brew. It's hard taming our flesh and not bowing to all its cravings. Yet, the more time we spent in prayer, the less significant the coffee was. Sometimes the coffee pot would automatically shut off before I even poured the first cup. I'm talking two hours later, and yet the time flew by. We would experience the presence of God, see prayers answered, and grow closer together as husband and wife. The Lord would burden our hearts on an issue and lead us to Scripture that would seem to just leap off the page. It was amazing how my wants were changed, too. Yes, if we want to see a change, we have to do the work, but it is so worth it! We were witnessing Psalm 17:6, "I have called upon You, for You will hear me, O God; Incline Your ear to me, and hear my speech." When I speak, I want to be heard and understood. It still baffles my mind that the

God of the Universe really hears me, along with everyone else, on this vast earth that calls upon His Name. The Lord was sustaining our prayer life.

 Father, cause me to see the supernatural in the natural, in Jesus' name.

6

The Prayer of
A Righteous Man Avails Much

As our spiritual life was growing, so was our involvement at church. We wanted to serve and felt that we had been given so much that we had to give back. It wasn't out of religious duty, but out of the love we received that we wanted to help others.

Our church was a very mission-oriented church, both at home and abroad. Our pastor had a heart for missions and it was shared by most of the congregation. Missions began in our family, as our oldest child was the first one out of the gate to serve in New Orleans after Hurricane Katrina in 2006. Michael had made new friends at church and was now a part of the youth group. Many of them had signed up for this trip, and we thought it would be a life-changing experience for him. Michael spent his entire spring break helping strangers, which was a huge sacrifice for a teenager. I was proud of him for being so selfless and putting others first. I remember the stories of devastation that he shared with us and the powerful effect it had on his heart. It opened his eyes to the real pain and suffering of others. A seed had been planted.

Mike just wanted to share what the Lord had done in his life with anyone who would listen, and his servant's heart was expanding rapidly. So I could understand his curiosity about attending an informational meeting about a possible missions trip to India. We weren't missionaries and certainly didn't travel outside the country, except for our twentieth wedding anniversary trip. Heck, we were just getting our family straightened out and on the right path. What harm could this meeting possibly do?

"I don't hear any India for you!" Yep, that was the first statement out of my mouth when Mike came home from the missions meeting at church and nonchalantly announced that he wanted to go to India. When he discussed the details of the trip, I thought he was insane. I finally had the husband I longed for and enjoyed being with, and now he wanted to go off to some God-forsaken land. This was not in *my* framework for our nice, little, church-abiding family. We had gone through so many trying times financially in the past, and the fear of lack was presenting itself front and center. I felt like I was just catching my breath from the past years of ups and downs. Yes, Jesus had carried me through those times, but I was enjoying the respite of peace and tranquility. Mike told me about an arrow piercing his heart as talk about India unfolded during the meeting. Well, there's no way my self-employed, electrician husband was going halfway around the world to a dangerous place where his life could be in jeopardy. I felt an arrow hit, too. It hit my stomach and not my heart, and I didn't like it one bit. I was finally enjoying being with him and now God wanted to send him away? It just didn't make sense to me, but I would soon learn that following God doesn't always make sense.

India was now beginning to compete for our time, talents and treasures. India was a new mission field for our church and uncharted land. It would be a scouting trip in both the north and south regions of the country. Yes, we did have contacts on the ground, but our team would still be on their own, traveling in an unknown country without an interpreter until they reached their destination. Also, it would be very evident with their ivory skin tones that they were not nationals. It would take several months for me to start seeing the calling of God on this groundbreaking trip. Every time someone mentioned India, I would have this sinking feeling in my stomach. I really just wanted to put my fingers in my ears and say, "I can't hear you, I can't hear you!" as if that would magically make the whole trip just vanish into thin air.

The team was made up of five people: three women, Pastor Bill and Mike. The ladies were going to help others set up businesses and do some fun Bible teachings with the kids at the orphanage. Pastor Bill was going to speak at a pastors' conference on the grounds while Mike was going to be running electric for the computer lab at the children's school. As a fairly new Christian, his missions experience was zero, but his zeal for the Lord was a ten.

It would not be long before the finances were coming in for the team and the plans were falling into place. The trip would be fifteen days long. Fifteen days without contact from anyone on the team and no father presence in the home. Fifteen days of three kids, aged five, thirteen, and seventeen. I had never been left alone with our kids for that long. Also, the fact that Mike was a self-employed contractor and I was a stay-at-home mom left me feeling very concerned. If Mike was not working, there was no income. His vacation time was not paid. Would he lose all his customers because he wasn't here to service them and they would call someone else? How was this going to affect us financially? What would happen if someone had an electrical emergency? I had recently read a horrific encounter of missionaries being killed and not returning home to their loved ones. All these negative thoughts kept swirling around in my head. Yes, they were negatives which would normally not be attributed to the hand of God, but they also were hard core facts that I could not ignore.

I always thought that I had a gift of faith, but this was just taking me to new heights I could not have imagined. My tent pegs were being pulled up and extended way beyond what I could see. My ropes were stretched to the point where I felt they would snap. I could not stop God's plan. I proceeded out of obedience to support this uncomfortable calling for Mike. Only then did I start to see God's stamp of approval when finding a pair of men's size eleven sandals in the store. What's the big deal about that? Stores carry size eleven sandals all summer. This just happened to be October! Yep, the *only* pair of sandals left on the rack just happened to be Mike's size. The Lord had them sitting there waiting for our purchase, because everyone wears sandals in the winter months in Delaware with cold temperatures and possible snow, right? It was another opportunity to thank God for His plan and provision regarding this assignment.

After months of preparation, the time had now come for the commissioning of the team. It would include a family and team meal together at a restaurant and going to the prayer chapel at church for a foot washing ceremony and prayer. The foot washing is a very powerful time, as each team member demonstrates what Jesus did for His own. It brings such unity and humility to the team. Afterwards, Pastor Bill had us join in a circle, holding hands for prayer. He said he felt someone had a word for the team. The room was silent. Everyone waited patiently for what God wanted to say.

Amazingly, I had a scripture burning in my heart. It was Psalm 20: 7, "Some trust in chariots and some in horses, but we trust in the name of the Lord our God." It certainly was the scripture I was clinging to for this trip, so I remained silent, thinking it was only for me. Pastor Bill asked again if someone had a word. My hands were now sweaty and shaking and the Word was churning within me, so I responded with the verse. Hey, it's God's Word and it's up to Him to do with it what He chooses! The service ended and we dispersed to our homes. There were so many other "kisses from Heaven," that by the time I dropped Mike off at the train station, he had my full support. I was still concerned, but I had a peace in my heart that Mike would be okay. The other apprehensive women in his life also blessed the trip. My mom and his mother had released Mike, which we know was only by the grace of God.

After the team returned home, Mike was so excited to share with me what happened with that word. When the team arrived at the orphanage in Bapatla, it was very late at night. As they drove through the iron gates onto the property, the children were all lined up to greet the new American visitors. With bright, smiling faces, they were joyfully singing a song with the words, "Some trust in chariots and some horses, but we trust in the name of the Lord." Wow! My socks were just blown off when I heard that! I was so glad that I did not keep that verse to myself, thinking it was only for me. You can imagine how the team must have felt, hearing the confirming word after many long days of travel in a foreign land. I was happy that I overcame the fear of man and spoke up. God is so faithful!

The word also helped stabilize Mike as the trip was full of challenges and events that would have made the average man buckle. He was given a water bottle that had been deceptively refilled with unfiltered tap water, unbeknownst to him, and became extremely ill. His room was robbed of all his cash and he had to rely on the team to help him. He had ignorantly walked through a Hindu temple and became sick for ten months with lung issues. The area was so spiritually oppressive that it was physically affecting the other team members, causing them to vomit. It was not an expedition for the faint of heart, yet it became the first of ten other subsequent trips back to Asia.

Before the India trip was even on the radar, the church had partnered with a fantastic organization called Amazon Medical Missions that was founded by Mike and Susie Dempsey. Pastor Bill was introduced to them years before he pastored Immanuel and had established a strong relationship with these faithful servants of Jesus. Their mission was to serve the poor of Peru that lived on the Amazon River and its many tributaries. They built an incredible riverboat that had a fully equipped operating room, along with multiple sleeping quarters and a dining room to house huge teams. It was a first class operation that the Dempseys had built from the ground up, leaving the comforts of the U.S. to provide medical care and the Gospel to the Peruvians. Our church sent many teams to support the Dempseys and I was happy to have my feet planted here in the States to be a prayer intercessor for the teams. A year later, my second born son Steven signed up to go and included his dad.

Oh boy! I loved that my teen wanted to serve, but we had just come out of a difficult year financially. Now, more stress would be put on our pocketbooks. Again, I would walk through a test of faith for all needs to be met, not knowing what the Lord had planned for the future.

The following year rolled around and the Peru trip was once again presented to us. This time it wasn't just two going -- the whole family wanted to go! We were talking about big buckaroos for a family of five. When we calculated the cost, it would have been cheaper to fly to Disney World for a week and stay in one of the upscale resorts in the park. We did give the kids a choice between Disney and Peru and all were in favor of Peru, except Ashley, who was seven at the time. Who could blame her for wanting the all-American dream vacation of Disney World that most kids long for? Even though Ashley was ultimately outnumbered, I was thrilled when the Lord blessed her with a Disney opportunity four years later. Even so, it didn't take long for her to get on board to the great adventure that was before us.

It was a rich time preparing our hearts, minds and body to serve. We take for granted the clean living conditions of our nation, along with access to top medical facilities. Part of our preparations were making sure all our immunizations were up to date. We also had designated homework assignments so the team would be educated on the weather, culture, government and monetary exchange rates. Knowledge is power and keeps you safe from making costly mistakes. Our pastor was excellent at identifying the team members' strengths and weaknesses. He also assigned us different ministry positions where we would be apt to succeed. No one wants to serve if frustration and failure are the main results. It is already stressful traveling to a foreign nation where there are language barriers and in the case of Peru, extreme jungle heat. I can remember sweating in places I never thought you could.

The Lord met our financial needs and I tried to keep my eyes locked on Him as various challenges presented themselves. We experienced all sorts of bizarre occurrences, from our bedroom TV turning itself on at four a.m. the day we were leaving for Peru, to our daughter Ashley being choked by an evil spirit in the airport returning home. God demonstrated His power and love during the entire trip. We were also shown His great mercy as three of the five of us ignorantly enjoyed a frozen treat, cooling off from the sticky jungle humidity before the long journey home. After the last refreshing gulp, I realized what we had done. Ice is still water that is not filtered and carries bacteria. We were in big trouble! The prayers started immediately that we would not have any ill effects from the slushies. We were also taking supplements to calm our stomachs. God answered our prayers to get us safely home without emergency bathroom visits, but as soon as we crossed the threshold of our house, let's just say I was extremely grateful we had three toilets. The temporary discomfort we experienced was well worth the love for missions the Lord wrote on our hearts that trip.

The mission field is a crazy place that messes up your preconceived ideas of what the world looks like and how things should be. As human beings, we all need food, shelter and clothing. The basics that we don't even think about on a day-to-day basis are luxuries to most of the world. I was shocked to learn that only twenty-five percent of the world actually has running water in their homes. That means seventy-five percent do not. Have you ever thought about that? Are you counted in that twenty-five percent? I shudder to think about all the water I nonchalantly wasted while letting the faucet run while brushing my teeth. I think about all the gallons from the extra-long, hot showers that I took because, well, I could, or a bubble bath when I wasn't even dirty. How about running the washing machine with only half a load because I wanted to wear something that was in the laundry basket and didn't want to wait for a full load? How much water have I wasted washing cars or hosing down the driveway because it looked dirty? I think about the times when the water company was flushing out the pipes and I would temporarily lose water pressure and quickly become angry. Lord, forgive my self-centeredness and frivolous waste as I did not think about the seventy-five percent less fortunate who do without every single day.

Jesus said that the poor would always be among us, but we are not to misuse what has been given to us. It is the things like the gift of water that compel me to give back and serve the less fortunate. I am so grateful for indoor plumbing, western toilets and all our modern conveniences. It's sometimes hard to believe that most people do not live the same way. When Mike came home from India the very first time, he suffered from overwhelming guilt from the blessed life we lived. After a hot shower of washing off the filth of a third world country, the unworthiness of having a box spring and mattress to sleep on was wrestling him to the floor, literally. He just couldn't bring himself to sleep in our bed without tremendous guilt. Obviously, I could not relate to the extreme poverty he had witnessed for three weeks, but I was reminded that God determines the exact places where we should live (Acts 17:26). We had no choice in where or when we were born, so I became a little frustrated that I finally had my bedmate home and he wanted to sleep on the floor. After a scolding from me that he needed to be grateful for the bed God provided for us, Mike finally returned to his side of the bed. The culture shock had a profound effect on us as we would witness poverty around the world.

 Father, how do You want me to serve the poor and needy? Give me Your heart for the hurting, in Jesus' name.

7

Who Is Your Provider?

J ust when you think you have it all figured out, the Lord allows events to happen so that we can see what we *truly* believe. Here is one that I'm sure the Lord chuckled about. We were preparing to go to India again. Three of us were going and we thought it would be much cheaper than the year before because we were only going to the south, whereas the year before included the north. We had someone call us asking for prayer that they also would be able to collect funds and go, too. Not a problem, we would ask Father God. We love praying for people and seeing how God will answer. The problem was that they wanted *our* main donor to give them the funds! My heart sank. Really? You want us to pray that our donor (who at the time had not yet supported us financially) will support you? Yikes! Immediately, I thought, "Lord, I don't like this!" Geez, I hate conflict, but this conflict was within myself.

Little remnants of orphan mindsets were trying to reat-tach and cause a feeling of fear, lack and doubt. I did not want to attempt to control and manipulate circumstances to feel safe and secure. Right away, I was convicted. I began to take captive my thoughts and ask myself who my provider was: God or man? Who was my God? Jesus or one of our donors? Who was my Father that loved me and cared about my needs? Oh, how ugly it is when we become possessive in the body of Christ! I repented quickly for relying on man and making him my source, doubting God and His provision for me. It is much easier to trust the One who owns the cattle on a thousand hills (Psalms 50:10). The Lord will never run out of provision for His children when we are in His will; yet, we can easily fall prey to the father of lies. It is too easy to listen to the voices of opposition when we are not feeding on the Word of God.

Look at Adam & Eve. They were accustomed to speaking with the Lord in the garden and walking with Him in the cool of the day. His voice was not strange or unfamiliar. Yet, the words of a snake persuaded them to doubt and disobey their Creator and consequently evict them out of their beautiful garden home. The words of doubt caused them to separate from the Lover of their souls. The fruit was speaking to them as well; not in an audible voice, but the Word tells us that it was pleasing to the eye. Do you not think their mouths were watering as they gazed upon the unblemished fruit? Oh, look around you. Everything is speaking to us; the dust on the bedroom end tables or the dirty laundry and dishes accumulating in our homes. The chocolate chip cookies in the kitchen cabinet are beckoning your name and the ice cream in the freezer screams to be devoured. Even the television tells-a-vision; where to shop, what your family should look like, how your body should be shaped, and what you should eat and drink. How about that mirror we gaze into every morning? What is that saying to you? I'll take a guess that it is more negative than positive! How about when we're out and about? Yep, I "hear" the billboards. I "hear" the fast food restaurants vying for my attention to just drive right through. What about you? Who is calling you? Who are you listening to? Whose voice defines you?

When I finally shut up the father of lies and turned my attention to my faithful Father God, I was able to relax and actually sincerely pray for others. This is how Daddy wants His kids to behave. Totally trusting Him, instead of trying to manipulate and figure things out, sets us free and allows God to be God. What burdens have you picked up that you weren't meant to carry?   Today, give them to the only One who can take care of them.

I remember when Mike was going on his first missions trip to Malawi, Africa. We both heard clearly the call of the Lord for Mike to go. Even so, at that time, it did not lessen the stretching that would take place for me to see it come to fruition. Malawi was an extremely expensive trip that was not in our budget. It is one of the world's least-developed countries; therefore, accommodations and travel costs were exorbitant. We had paid the initial down payment to secure his airline ticket, but nothing else.

As we were praying together one morning, Mike heard the Lord say that He had it, meaning the Lord would provide the remaining balance of the trip. I was grateful, knowing our finances would not take another hit, but also very curious as to how it all would unfold. As the week was winding down, a call came in on Friday from the church office. Someone had generously dropped off a $5,000 check for the missions trip to be split between Mike and our pastor. *Five thousand dollars*! Wow! I know nothing is impossible with God, but I was not expecting an answer so quickly. Tears streamed down my face as I thought of God's awesome power and love for us. We rejoiced mightily and thanked God as we drove to the church to collect the funds. Yes, our God certainly "had it"! I need to make an important note that the individual who wrote the check was not giving out of his surplus, but heard the Lord telling him to sow into that trip. It reminded me of when Paul received a gift in Philippians 4:18, a sweet-smelling aroma, an acceptable sacrifice, well pleasing to God. The donation was pleasing to God because He was being honored, and resources were being invested into eternal things.

I also remember another instance when the Lord really showed me who was the boss. Mike had a long-term commercial customer who was having financial difficulties that were so bad that he was closing shop. Mike had completed some electrical work prior to this company going under, but had not yet been paid. Weeks had gone by, and still no payment for his services. How do you approach a company in distress, expecting that you will be a priority on their long list of creditors? We started praying.

One morning, while Mike was praying in the shower he felt the Lord say to him that he had not asked God to release His angels. Perplexed, Mike asked in prayer exactly what that meant. The Lord gently responded to Mike that he had not asked God to release His angels on Mike's behalf to collect the funds owed him. So out of faith, Mike asked God to release His angels to the bookkeeper so that she would not be able to get him off of her mind and the bill would be paid. Mike never said anything to me as he finished his morning routine and kissed me goodbye, going out the door to work. A couple hours later, the phone rang. When I answered, a woman introduced herself as the bookkeeper of the same company that was going bankrupt. She explained that Mike had done electrical work some time ago but she could not find his invoice, and…are you ready for this? She said she just could not get him off her mind! I knew we were praying for resolution, but the lady quoted Mike's prayer exactly. The invoice was paid in full.

 Father, help me to depend on You to meet all of my needs, in Jesus' name.

8

Trinidad, Our Isaac on the Island

We went through a huge testing of our faith and what I call our Isaac moment. A member of our church was from Trinidad, the southernmost island in the West Indies. She had many in her family who were practicing Hindus and asked our pastor if he and a team would go to share the Gospel. After much prayer, we agreed to go. Our connection with the people was immediate and actually quite overwhelming. Mike and I would soon make multiple trips, seeing God move in miraculous ways. We unexpectedly heard an undeniable calling from God to move there and serve one particular church. It was a heart-wrenching time for me, as I saw the internal pain it was causing all of us in the family. We would be leaving everything near and dear to us. Our family, friends, and church community would now be a five-hour flight away and we would be in a totally different country.

We committed to relocate and went as far as house hunting and checking out schools for Ashley. She was such a trooper as we navigated this foreign, tropical territory. Following God is not always easy and carefree. It comes with a great cost and we were ready to be obedient to what felt like an agonizing assignment. At least we thought we were. After many long expeditions, tears and a dark night of the soul, the door to go was shut. I truly felt as Abraham, when God tested him to sacrifice his son, Isaac. We were tested to be obedient to His call. I learned many excruciating lessons of releasing my will and trusting God completely during that anguishing time. It was an extremely tough season, but I'm grateful for all the experiences that helped me grow and mature in my Christian walk. I witnessed the hand of God not only moving in my life, but the lives of others as well.

On one of those ventures in Trinidad, Mike was going to do an introduction to missions and the Great Commission to go out and make disciples. Not long after he had begun his message, all the lights went out in the church. Funny how the lights went out in the building, but no one could put out the power of God. Mike continued speaking without missing a beat, as this was not the first time something like this had ever happened out in the field.

We had the privilege of teaching a group of evangelists the "EvangeCube", which is a puzzle-like evangelistic tool used to help tell the story of salvation through Jesus. It catches people's attention because it is a cube with illustrations on all sides that as you manipulate the cube, it draws people into the story. It is also fun to do when you learn how the pictures unfold in order. Sometimes when there is a language barrier and we are not always sure the interpreter is interpreting accurately, this cube allows the people to look at the picture and understand the correct message. We have found that the cube is obviously more effective when we incorporate our own testimony as well. We were also able to give a couple of cubes away to the pastor's daughters, who couldn't wait to take them to school. We heard the good news later that four people had received Christ as their Savior the following day! We also were able to demonstrate the EvangeCube at the girls' Christian high school. We never take for granted that the Gospel message can be preached anywhere, whether in a Christian environment or not. There are just too many people that are one decision away from making Heaven their forever home. When the demonstration was finished, many in the classroom were raising their hands for salvation. Praise the Lord!

Another interesting story was an encounter with a man who was staying on the island with family as he tried to settle his late brother's estate. The man's name was Uncle Johnny. He was an interesting man, Uncle Johnny. He was an accountant and also a Muslim. Not just any Muslim, but an esteemed leader of his faith in the community. He could quote the Koran, as well as the Bible. We began sharing about the Lord Jesus and His goodness to us. Uncle Johnny had talked about the Christians that he had known back home in Guyana. They would arrogantly walk down the street carrying their Bibles on a Sunday morning so others would know just where they were going: church. We know the types, praising God on Sunday, displaying their *holier than thou* attitude and then living a totally different life on Monday. I don't know who they think they are fooling, because most people know what is authentic and what is downright prideful and ugly.

As our conversation with Uncle Johnny continued, I reminded him of the Koran teaching that is taken from the Bible regarding Jesus and His virgin birth. Uncle Johnny nodded in agreement to the truth of Jesus' divine entry into the world. So I challenged him as to who fertilized the egg? He looked at me with his big brown eyes as the question swirled in his head. Mike then prayed out loud for Jesus to reveal Himself to Uncle Johnny right then and there. Immediately, we witnessed Uncle Johnny's countenance change right there at the kitchen table. No one touched him and no one prayed long, wordy prayers. Jesus, in His ever-so-gentle manner, showed up. The hardness of Uncle Johnny's face left and was replaced by a huge smile from ear to ear. Upon seeing the sudden change, Mike asked if he would like to receive Jesus as his Lord and Savior. "Yes," was the response from Uncle Johnny, and the entire room erupted into sheer joy and celebration.

The others in the room were Uncle Johnny's relatives, who had been praying for his conversion for twenty years! I easily understood praying for many years for a loved one not yet a part of God's kingdom. The tears of happiness flowed and praises of thanksgiving to Jesus for saving this lost soul were deafening. You would have thought someone won the Super Bowl, but this was even better. This was an eternal victory that had been won of a man transferred from the kingdom of darkness to the Kingdom of Light! It didn't stop there, either. Mike had asked if Uncle Johnny suffered from any physical pain in his body. The answer was yes, so we began to ask Jesus to heal those places. Again, Uncle Johnny's face lit up with excitement as he declared that the pain in his neck and knees was completely gone. Our God not only cares about our eternity but our present; the right here, right now moments. Jesus wants to be part of our entire existence. He cares! He cares about the smallest details of our life and the major, life-altering ones. There is nothing hidden from His sight or anything so miniscule that is not worthy of His full, undivided attention.

Father, sharpen my ears to hear and follow only Your voice, in Jesus' name.

9

You Can't Make That Up

This day in the fall of 2013 was not a typical day. Hours earlier, Mike had a tugging on his heart to go into the prayer chapel. He finished up his electrical job and obeyed the divine prompting. The small chapel was empty, like it usually was during the work week. As he began to pray, the Lord started downloading and he quickly grabbed a pen and paper. He was wondering how this message would fit into his life. Nothing jumped off the page, and so he left and continued on with his work day. When he came home, he told me what had happened. I was curious to hear why the Lord had burdened his heart and what was so important that the Lord would pull him off a job site to have his undivided attention. Mike read the letter out loud to me. I questioned how it was for him, as well.

Wednesday nights Mike, Ashley and I usually went to the mid-week prayer meeting at church. I thought it might be for someone coming that night or it would possibly tie into the theme for the evening. Mike neatly tucked the paper into his Bible. Nothing earth-shaking happened during prayer time and the word did not seem fit, so we actually kind of forgot about it. Mike and I were socializing with a few people afterwards and then proceeded to go home.

We were walking down the hallway when our daughter, Ashley, was coming towards us. There was a couple following closely behind her. Ashley asked us if we would pray for them. Apparently, they did not have an appointment scheduled for prayer with the Healing Rooms located upstairs and were turned away. Discouraged and desperate, they asked Ashley if she knew anyone who could pray for them. She knew exactly where to lead them and we were happy to serve. They were a husband and wife that looked like they had endured some rough battles. They were very fragile and the stale smell of cigarettes permeated their clothing. They tried to tell us their story, but we asked them to stop so we could hear what the Lord wanted to say regarding their situation. Their eyes widened. The pastor's wife and another prayer warrior joined us. We laid hands on the man, Larry, and started to pray.

Larry had confessed that he was sick and fighting cancer. We could see he was very weak as he leaned on his wife's arm for support. The lines on his face were deep and many. His feeble arms were so thin. My heart was filled with compassion for a man needing a touch from God. The intercessor had a word of knowledge that Larry was holding on to unforgiveness and that he had a broken heart. Immediately, tears welled up in his eyes as he told us about his teenage daughter's accident. She was paralyzed from a single car accident. She had hit a tree and it forever changed her world, along with that of her parents, who now cared for her. We ministered to the pain and disappointment that he carried entombed within his heart.

Minutes later, I saw Mike open his Bible and pull out the paper from earlier. I had completely forgotten about it! Mike began reading it out loud, "I have not forgotten you tonight." Not yesterday, not today, but *tonight*! What made that sentence so significant was that while we were downstairs ending our prayer time, Larry was upstairs in the Healing Rooms. He had come that night for prayer, but was turned away because he did not call ahead for an appointment and there was no opening available. Discouraged but determined, he and his wife shuffled downstairs just as people from our prayer meeting were heading to the parking lot. Ashley was waiting for us at the end of the hallway and overheard this couple asking for someone to pray for them. Ashley was quick to volunteer her parents, and led them to us at the other end of the hallway.

We were all encouraged by how the Lord showed Himself strong and compassionate towards Larry that night. We said goodbye and expected to hear a good report soon. The next time we heard from Larry's wife, the news was not good. Larry was in the hospital. He was not conscious when his family would visit him. Mike and I were determined to go pray for him. We just felt that the Lord was not quite finished with him yet. It was amazing that Larry was alone when we arrived at his hospital room. We were not able to communicate with him. He was apparently on a lot of pain medications. Mike and I prayed and left quietly. The next phone call informed us that Larry had indeed recovered and come home for a while, but now was on the hospice wing of a different hospital. We were eight days away from our missions trip to India. How could we expect God to show up in India if we didn't first believe He would be right here in our own hometown?

Mike and I had the faith for Larry to get well and walk out of that place. We went to see him and, again, no family members were present. It was as though the Lord cleared the room out for us to minister so that no presence of doubt and unbelief could interfere. Larry was more aware this time and could hold a conversation with us. He was fighting for survival and not ready to go to his heavenly home just yet. We prayed again, expecting good news upon our return from India. As we walked past the nurse's station, we had to sign out. Mike confidently made a bold comment that Larry would be going back home. The nurse smiled politely and said that they hoped that for everyone. Mike said, "No, you don't understand. Larry *is* going home."

The nurse just looked at us like we had two heads. She responded sarcastically, "Okay."

We had peace in our hearts to go to India, knowing that Larry was in God's hands. Weeks later after returning from our India trip, we still had not heard a word about Larry. My curiosity was getting the best of me and the voices in my head declaring Larry had died swirled about me. I have to admit that I did look up his name on the online obituary section of the newspaper. His name did not come up. I finally called his wife for a report. Larry had, indeed, recovered and was home with his family! Wow! God is good. I had to repent for my unbelief and for doubting the power of Jesus. Mike and I rejoiced at the goodness of the Lord.

Larry did eventually pass away, but even that event was amazing. Five months later, his wife Charlene called to tell us that Larry was again in hospice. This time it was at a different place. We would find out later that it just so happened to be the place where my daughter-in-law, Stephanie, just started working. She was his nurse. Charlene recognized Stephanie's last name on her name tag and began to inquire about who her parents were. Stephanie told her about her own mom and dad. Charlene finally asked, "Well, how did you get that last name?" They finally connected the dots back to us.

Stephanie was aware of Larry's story; she just didn't realize that this man was *the* Larry. What a joy to know that she would be comforting him during the last precious days of his earthly life. Mike was able to get in to see Larry and his family before his final departure. He truly died peacefully, knowing that God did not forget him.

Days later, we received another phone call from Charlene. While planning Larry's funeral, she wanted Mike and I there as a testament to what the Lord had done in the past year. She wanted to know if Mike was a pastor so that he could conduct the funeral. He was not, but we assured her that we would be in attendance and he would speak if she so desired.

At the funeral, it was amazing to see how many family members knew who we were by Larry's story. Mike was able to speak and declare the goodness of God and His faithfulness to each and every one of us. You just don't know how, where or when God is going to present Himself and we need to be ready in and out of season, like the Bible tells us in 2 Timothy 4:2. Larry's wife also gave the handwritten word back to us and it is a reminder of the kind of personal relationship God wants with His precious kids.

 Father, give me the boldness to conquer the fear of man and proclaim Your faithfulness, in Jesus' name.

10

Just Follow Your Husband

Following your husband certainly sounds easy enough if it's just for one time. Hopefully, if you are married, you have established enough trust in the relationship that this would not be an issue. I think back to the times when I did not follow my husband and instead yanked the reins of decision out of his hands abruptly without discussing the matter at all. I cringe at the times that I would take control because of doubt or fear of Mike's ability to make the correct choice. Yet, if the roles were reversed, I would not have been so gracious with the outcome.

I remember when I was the facilitator for our church's women's Bible study. Our curriculum consisted of Beth Moore's Bible studies. Our group had completed most of them over a period of many years. You can imagine my excitement upon hearing that Beth would be coming to little old Delaware for a Living Proof Live Event! Even though Delaware was the first state to ratify the Constitution of the United States, many think it's a city and not an actual state. It's not a place that draws many to hold concerts or host well-known people.

The conference was announced nine months in advance. I couldn't wait to share the news with Mike that my "mentor" would be visiting our home state and that I really wanted to attend. Much to my surprise, Mike expressed an interest to go, as well. I was ecstatic that I would be able to share that experience with my husband. We both enjoyed Beth's teaching, whether we watched her on TBN (Trinity Broadcast Network) or the DVDs from the weekly Bible study that I would review at home while preparing for class. We decided that we would make a date night out of it, enjoying dinner together before the conference. Nine months seemed like an eternity, but I just spent the time imagining sitting in the front row and gleaning more wisdom from this powerhouse of a teacher.

As the date approached, our plans were made to eat at a restaurant right down the street from the arena so I could be there early to get my front row seat. Upon finishing our meal, we hopped in the car, full of excitement and anticipation. When we reached the destination, I felt this angry rage overtake me. There was already a long line halfway around the building! How could this happen? We arrived early, but obviously not early enough. I started flipping out and complaining that those people already in line were going to take *my* cherished, front row seat. I guess Delaware wasn't as small and unpopular as I thought. Mike calmly drove around the full parking lot, looking for the best spot. I could feel the daggers coming out of me as I urged him to park quickly because more people were joining the line, thus knocking me further back from *my* seat. He told me to just relax and that God had the perfect seats for us. Oh yes, they were the perfect seats, all right -- with other people sitting in them!

We finally parked. I swung open my car door quickly so I could run to the end of the line, which by this time was at the back of the building. I began to scan the crowd and it was at that moment that I realized all the attendees were women. I knew that Beth was primarily a women's Bible teacher, but it never crossed my mind that no men would attend. The Word of God is the Word of God regardless of who is teaching, at least for me. I immediately apologized to Mike that he was the only male there. It didn't bother him in the least.

As we proceeded toward the rear, a long, strong, muscular arm came out from the stream of people and grabbed Mike. It was another male, apparently not so secure in being a minority in the vast sea of estrogen. He invited us to stand in line with him. My spirit jumped for joy, since he was somewhat closer to the main doors than where the line ended. My gracious husband declined, reassuring the man that he would be all right. I literally could have killed him. I believed it was a divine setup to get me to my front row seat, and he squashed it like a grape. With my head bowed low in defeat, we took our place in the back of the line.

Women were chatting all around us and you could feel the excitement in the air. I was still trying to figure out how we would be able to get in the front row despite our dreadful position at the moment. All of a sudden, a woman in front of us turned around and asked Mike in a sarcastic tone, "Who did you come to see?" I was appalled that she would think my man was there to just check out all the ladies.

Without missing a beat, he responded, "I came to see Jesus!" He added that he believed the Lord told him that He wanted to deal with the heart.

"Oh really, that's what God told you?" She quickly turned back around to her group. It's amazing how rude the body of Christ can be to their own. I smiled at Mike and marveled at his quick response, not being rattled by such a mocking display.

Eventually, the doors opened and the line began to move. I told Mike that once we got in, he should go directly to the front row since he was tall and would be able to find seats up close. As we were nearing the front, more women were waiting to join the line. Mike graciously let them go ahead of us. I was, again, flipping out. How could he let others get in the way of me and my seat? Once our tickets were scanned, he entered the seating area. By the time I reached him, he signaled that all the seating on the floor had been taken. Of course all those seats were gone! It was a no-brainer with all the people he had let go before us in line. He headed up the stairs on the side seating of the platform. I was desperately looking for seats on the floor that maybe he had missed.

When I looked up to see where he was, Mike was pointing to two seats at the end of the row, half way up from the floor level. There were two seats in the same section that were two rows closer to the stage that I wanted, but he would not move. He signaled to me that he wanted the end seat. I just stood there, pointing to my seats while he stood his ground, insisting on his spot. When I realized I was not getting my way and how foolish I was behaving, I moved up to his seats. Oh, I was so miserable. Since we were on the end, I had to stand up every time someone wanted to sit in our row. Mike would just smile at me, making me even more mad.

When I was sitting, all I could do was stare in jealousy and anger at the people in my front row seats. I didn't wait nine months to sit in these horrible seats. Some women from our

Bible study group showed up in our section looking for seats but decided they wanted seats elsewhere, so they moved to another section. After stewing for a while, a conviction of ungratefulness came sweeping over me. The Lord reminded me that I could have been at home missing this entire event, and how it was an honor and blessing to be there, regardless of my seating. I began to repent for my selfishness and pride. I felt the peace of Christ fill me and my joy return. I began to notice that there were banners all over the auditorium advertising the latest Bible study about a woman's heart. Hmm, I guess Mike was hearing God. I could see familiar faces from my church group directly across from us as they waved.

The lights dimmed and the worship team began playing. We stood on our feet, praising our great God! I felt like I had entered the throne room of Heaven as the music ushered in the presence of God. "Enter His gates with thanksgiving and His courts with praise," is the scripture in Psalms 100:4, and we were doing it.

When the worship had ended, the lights were brought up. I could see this tiny, little blond walk up onto the platform and grab the microphone. I was so excited to finally see my favorite Bible teacher in the flesh. She addressed the crowd, thanking us for coming, thinking that no one would really know her in Delaware and she was surprised at the numbers that showed up. She wasn't the only one! Beth revealed that this was her first time in our small state as she headed toward the stairs into the audience. My eyes got bigger as I watched her walk right passed the front row and head towards my side of the building. I couldn't believe it as she started up the stairs in my section. I was in complete shock, fumbling with my flip phone to try and snap a picture. I had promised my daughter Ashley a photo since I thought I would be in the front row with an unobstructed view.

Beth stopped halfway up the stairs and engaged a young woman with some questions. I was like a star-crazed groupie. I didn't even hear what she asked; I was just in amazement. I thought I had seen it all until she proceeded to move up the stairs even closer to us. I think my chin hit the ground when she stopped at the row in front of us and shimmied past the women seated on the end to the woman directly in front of me. She had a conversation with her for a couple of minutes, not hurrying through the tragic story of recently losing a loved one. I could see the real compassion in her eyes, since we were practically breathing the same air. Beth always jokes about her big Texas hair, but she is such a tiny thing and so beautiful right down to her polished toenails peeking out her high heeled pumps. I know because I checked her out from top to bottom.

As I glanced over to Mike in complete awe, I noticed one of the two jumbotrons with these huge familiar faces on it -- ours! I wanted to die. I was there to see Beth and not have my mug on the wall for all to see. Then, as she moved back to the aisle, still talking to the crowd, Beth noticed Mike. She looked right at us and then put her hand on his shoulder and addressed him as her guy friend. I don't know what our faces must have looked like, but she then leaned over to Mike and quietly said that she hoped that she had not embarrassed him and that she was only there to serve. Beth Moore, my Bible teacher hero, was touching my man, calling him "guy friend" and concerned about embarrassing him! I didn't think I could love her any more! Needless to say, God *did* have the perfect seats for us. Afterwards, the other women from the group were a little disappointed that they didn't sit with us. I have since learned to let Mike pick our seats wherever we go!

I'm sad to say that wasn't the first time Mike was so confident in our seat selection. Years prior, Jesse Duplantis was in the area for a speaking engagement. We had seen him on TV many times and were interested in attending. A group of five of us decided to go together. On the way to the venue I realized that we weren't going to be the early birds, and I started getting nervous about our seating. We didn't have tickets with assigned seats, and being short and sitting in the back is not ideal. I prayed out loud in our minivan for the power of agreement. I prayed for God's favor for a decent parking spot and seats. Right away, Mike corrected me and thanked the Lord for our front row seats. Okay, that sounded good to me, but as we pulled into the parking lot that was pretty full, I really didn't see that prayer being fulfilled.

Mike dropped us off at the door and he parked the vehicle. Once he met up with us inside, we proceeded to find five empty seats that were together. I headed towards the back where there were still some vacant chairs available, but Mike was walking in the opposite direction, towards the front. When he reached the front row, five people stood up. Mike politely asked them if they were leaving, and they responded yes. I was shocked as my husband waved us forward to the front row to claim our "reserved" seats. I just couldn't understand how five people would sit in the front row until minutes before an event would begin and then just stand up and walk away. I still don't understand what happened that day. Who knows? Maybe they were angels, saving our seats. I was disappointed that I didn't get to see them personally and check for wings somehow concealed beneath their clothing.

After I had gotten saved, I had this mindset that Mike's decisions would not be correct because he was not hearing the leading of the Lord. As I look back now at some of the decisions that were made then, I see where I was greatly deceived. God still uses people -- the good, bad, saved and unsaved. He's looking for obedience, and not necessarily what makes sense or looks good to man. I'm just reminded of Noah building the ark. Noah wasn't the typical man. The Scriptures tell us that Noah walked with God, but there is no mention of his wife's relationship with God. What was she thinking when Noah informed her of his latest assignment? I can't imagine the conversations he must have had with his wife. I know I would have been asking a million questions, like, "Are you sure you heard correctly? Are you positive you are to be spending all your precious time building something that we may never use or have truly ever seen? What are all the neighbors going to think? There are so many other things you could be doing around the house."

I would have come up with a hundred different uses for the freshly cut lumber. I can just imagine the palace that could have been constructed or the expanding and updating of our original housing.

Or, what do you think the conversations with his grown sons sounded like? Did they have the same faith as their dad? Did they complain day after day, month after month as they labored to erect this strange monstrosity in the backyard? Just getting my family members to take out the trash could sometimes be a chore. Ham, Shem and Japheth would have needed to be not only dedicated to their father, but dedicated to their God as well.

Are we that dedicated to follow through on instructions from our Heavenly Father that may take blood, sweat and many years? I didn't always want to stay in a painful relationship. Sometimes I felt as though it did require all my blood, sweat, tears and many years. Yet, I did not have a release in my spirit to leave. I did not have peace to pack up and get out. What kept me here? My Sustainer. Sure it would have been easier to listen to others on the outside and to not have to deal with some of the unpleasantries. The world is all for the, "If it feels good, do it," mentality. No one wants to do the hard work of fighting for marriage and family.

Why did you stay in your marriage? It's a question I hear often. The world encourages self-protection and standing up for yourself. I'm not saying anyone should stay in an abusive relationship where their life is in danger. I'm talking about laying our wants down for the sake of others. People need to truly see what that looks like, up close and personal. It's easy to stick with someone through life when there are occasional bumps in the road. How about mountains? Mountains where you can't see the peak to climb up over and move on. Mountains that are so high and wide they seem impassable. What do we do then? Jesus tells us that He will never leave us, nor forsake us. Okay, so I won't climb that mountain alone, but it's still a big mountain. He also says that He won't give us more than we can handle. So I'm capable of conquering this obstacle. When I lay down what I want, when I make Jesus the center of my life and focus only on Him, the journey begins. What the Lord was showing me once I decided to proceed forward was that the road was very wide at the bottom of the mountain. Wide enough for others to travel along with me. Wide enough for not only the ones who would encourage me to go farther, but for others who would discourage and hinder me from reaching my next destination. Can you identify the ones in your life who are either prodding you along or pushing you back? Some of the intentions of the travelers aren't quite revealed until further along in the journey and some of the travelers are present for only a season and some for the long haul.

The Lord was also showing me a guardrail along this road. The guardrail represented the Word of God that would keep me centered on the will of God so that I would not veer to the left or to the right, but stay centered. I don't know how many times I have hit that guardrail, either because I didn't like what was on the road or was trying to take a shortcut thinking, "I know best." I typically would not just graze the guardrail, but proceed full steam ahead and experience a direct hit, head on. Even though it hurt, I'm so thankful for the corrections of the Lord. It is so much less painful than if I were left to my own way. Yes, even after a full on collision with the guardrail, healing occurred at a much faster rate with the Lord's safety measures in place. Hebrews 12:11 tells us, "Now no chastening seems to be joyful for the present, but painful; nevertheless, afterward it yields the peaceable fruit of righteousness to those who have been trained by it." Pain is a good teacher so as to not miss or repeat the lesson.

As I continue climbing upward, the road takes a sharp turn so the way is no longer visible. Will I continue without physically seeing the way? I am reminded that the Word is a lamp unto my feet. I also notice that some of my companions have abandoned me. It's amazing how the harder and steeper the walk is, the more it sifts out the ones not as committed to the call. I understand that some can only go so far. Not everyone's call is the same or should look the same. We serve a God who is too creative and limitless to make us all like cookie cutters. I'm so grateful that we serve a God who will meet us right where we are! I am learning to appreciate all the different gifts in the body of Christ. There are times where I admire someone else's gift, like singing. Earphones and a karaoke machine proved that I am to take a big step away from that one! Let's just say it is not very nice, according to my lovely family; although I believe it could heal some, since the Word declares that laughter is good medicine! Yet, I know my King is pleased with me as His Word says "make a joyful noise unto the Lord," (Psalm 100:1). He is the only One who truly appreciates my noise. Still, I am not in competition with or jealous of others who excel in this musical gift. So this adventurous journey continues.

As we continue to follow the leading of the Lord, I am overwhelmed by how the Lord was using us; from speakers at multiple prayer breakfasts to facilitating a women's Bible study, to global missions. We have served in Asia, Africa, and Europe, as well as South America and the islands. Our lessons were learned on the field in the midst of the battle. We have spent years training and healing from past wounds. Our scars are many, and I'm thankful for how the Lord continues to use them for His glory. We now have the privilege of ministering, healing and deliverance as we walk through the guts and glory of peoples' lives, partnering with the Divine Healer.

 Father, teach me to submit to You and those You have placed in authority over me, in Jesus' name.

11

He Will Not Share His Glory

For many years, I innocently took all the credit for praying my husband into an eternity in Heaven. It was easy to garner sympathy and accolades from others as this heroic wife who diligently prayed for thirteen years and God answered. Thirteen years of tears, sorrow and heartache finally turned into healing, joy and restoration. My story was encouraging to others who were desperate and hurting and I was more than happy to share it. As time went by, however, I had an unsettling feeling in my soul. As I looked back at what unfolded, it was revealed to me that it was God's story. The words I prayed were, "As he uses his mouth to curse your Kingdom, Lord, may he use his mouth to bless your Kingdom." Now that sounds nice and dandy and all, but truly that was *not* the prayer of *my* heart.

Yes, as a child of God, I wanted to see the Kingdom of God expand, but honestly, I first and foremost wanted a man that would be a more loving husband to me and a greater dad to my children. I wanted all the worldly views of the perfect marriage which, of course, I now know don't exist. I wanted the godly order in our home where Mike would love and be loved without addiction being part of the picture. I desired for Mike to be the spiritual leader of our home and a godly example to our children. My focus was on my own little world and family that seemed to be crumbling all around me. I was desperate for peace and comfort in place of storms and turmoil. Every time I retold the story, I felt God nudging me saying, "Really? That was your prayer? That was your true desire?" Yet, where did that prayer come from that so easily flowed from my lips?

The Bible tells us that when we ask for anything that is in accordance to His will, it is done. So obviously, Mike's conversion was His will for the way it unfolded and continues to this day. Yes, His will that I prayed was answered, but it took thirteen years for the fulfillment. I often wondered why there was such a delay. I know God doesn't waste anything, including time. That's how long it took to get my focus off of Mike and my circumstances and onto the real project: me. The thirteen years was for my training and equipping so that I would be prepared for what God was going to do in my family. All those years, I blamed Mike for not getting with the program and making life so difficult. Geez, it's so ugly when the blinders are removed and you can really see the problem.

When you have a victim mentality, you always blame others and never examine yourself. It's so easy to point the finger and not take responsibility for our own choices when we don't like the results. Yet, God loves us so much He will use whatever motivates us to draw closer to Him. If I had had a happy-go lucky life with no conflicts or hiccups, I know that I would not have pursued a relationship with God. I needed a loud wake-up call to discover who I truly was, and to discover the God who was pursuing me. Who was this loving and patient God who ever-so-gently convicted me of taking His glory? The whole process just endeared me to Him even more. When we are the masters of our own lives and believe we are the center of the universe, why would we ever need God? If we don't recognize who God is, His characteristics, and His plan for our lives, how can we truly know who we are?

A child typically resembles his or her parents. Just think of some of the kids you know. If we don't know our Creator, our Father, how then can we possibly know who we are? My kids know who their parents are. Why? They have spent a lot of time with us. They know that they were born because we wanted to expand our family. We wanted to share our love and lives with our own flesh and blood. They understand that they are not here to be our slaves or serve us. Their purpose to be born was for us to love and nurture them. It has only been through intentional communication and countless hours together that these precious relationships have developed and continue to evolve. They have picked up some of our behaviors, good and bad. They have some of our same likes and dislikes. They have some of our same facial expressions and mannerisms. They carry our name. They have complete access to us and our home. Their positions as our sons and daughter are secure because of who they are and not based on their performance.

It is the same way with my Heavenly Father. If I don't spend time with Him, I will never know what pleases Him or what grieves Him. Yes, God has emotions. Remember, we are made in His image. He is not made into ours, which is what we so easily think. We mistakenly believe that God likes what we like and behaves like us. We believe if something is good in our eyes, then God will feel the same way. I think back to some of the earlier decisions I made in life that I thought were good and see now that they were not so good. Scripture tells us that His ways are not our ways and His thoughts are high above our thoughts. He also sees the entire picture, from start to finish. I am still learning to trust, even if it doesn't look good. If God ordained it, it's good. We walk by faith and not by sight. God loves me and He's got my back. I carry His name and He will guide me and protect me all the days of my life. This is so comforting to me. I began to repent for my pride and thank Him for all that He did, and His perfect love washed me clean.

Even though those were the hardest years of my life, I would not trade them for anything. I not only developed a love for the Word of God through Bible study but I developed a deep relationship with Jesus. He truly became my Husband and my Father, as the Scripture says. I was learning that being number one carries a lot of responsibility and I didn't have the power or strength to do it. It was learning to come to the place of total surrender. I say *learning*, because it's not natural for most people. I had been living in such a cycle of shame, fear and control that surrender was not part of my vocabulary. I had to relinquish control of my husband, kids, friends and family. Slowly, my focus had to be on Jesus and no one else.

I had to have dove's eyes. Doves don't have peripheral vision, so their gaze is locked straight ahead with no distractions from the left or right. I had to have my focus locked on Jesus. Again, it takes time when you're used to being a people pleaser who is always checking others' responses. I had to allow God to be my first love. I had to allow His opinion and His voice to be the loudest in my life. It's no different than when you're in a healthy marriage; when your spouse speaks, you're attentive to their voice. His direction for my life had to

he will not share his glory

hold the most weight. The only thing that makes all of this possible is trust.

I'll never forget the day Mike learned that we are not going to be together as husband and wife in Heaven. We were having a casual conversation in the kitchen and I made the comment that it will be great when we are in Heaven because we won't be married. He looked at me strangely. I went on to explain that according to Matthew 22:30, at the resurrection people will neither marry nor be given in marriage; they will be like the angels in Heaven. Mike actually started tearing up. I thought he would be happy not to be tied down to me for eternity, but the thought of us not being together in marriage saddened him. Again, only a move of God on his heart would have triggered such a reaction. I began to explain that he would still know me, but it will be so much greater than our relationship now. How? I can't say. I only believe what the Word tells me, and it is that I will be totally happy. As it is written, "Eye has not seen, nor ear heard, nor have entered into the heart of man the things which God has prepared for those who love Him," (1 Corinthians 2:9). I'm also comforted by the words of Jesus when He told His disciples that He was going to prepare a place for them (John 14:3). I'm glad I have many things to look forward to by not knowing all the answers now. I just know that I serve a God full of awe and wonder and He wants to share it all with me!

 Father, I thank You for Your patience and Your mercy that is new each day. I give You permission to change me so I look more like You, in Jesus' name.

12

He Is The Prize

Are you a conduit for Christ or a dam for the devil? That was a question the Lord asked me as I struggled to write this book. It's easy for me to talk about the goodness of God, but trying to get it on paper was a challenge. Why? The purpose of this book is to declare the glory of God in a broken life and to help others taste and see the goodness of the Lord in the land of the living. It is to give hope to the hopeless when it looks dark and desperate and to show the sudden actions of God that can change your life in a heartbeat. It is meant to demonstrate God's faithfulness, even when we are not faithful. It is to expose the lies that say: our situations are utterly hopeless, people will never change, and that addictions cannot be overcome. It is to bring life where everything looks dead, to set the captives free who are imprisoned, to heal the broken hearted, and open blinded eyes to our Almighty God and His awesome plan for us.

There are many "suddenlys" in the Bible, but most of the stories involve time. Don't get discouraged that God uses time. Yes, the devil would love to keep this story locked inside me.

Yet, the Scripture says that it is by the blood of the Lamb (Jesus) and the power of the testimony that men are set free. I'm busting that dam down today. I'm committed to sounding the trumpet that our God is not only real, but He is alive and active. Jesus is actively working on my behalf. If He is for me, then who can be against me?

How about you? Everyone has a story. Where have you seen God operating in your life? He is there. I'm just in awe that He first loved us, that even when I was an enemy to Him, God loved me. He loves you, too. The Word says that He does not favor one over another because we are all His favorite. All those that say *yes* to acknowledging Jesus Christ as the Son of God and the Lord of their lives experience abundant life, now and for eternity. Don't miss out on the greatest gift we can receive. With it comes His presence, His peace and His promises. When we go through the tough times in life, the Lord's arms are wide open, His eyes are locked on you, His ear is attentive to your prayers, and His thoughts of you are many. What are you waiting for? Don't let another minute go by without the assurance of securing your final destination once this brief life has passed, as well as living a life now full of His peace and guidance.

When I think of how God communicated with people before Christ came to the earth, I'm so thankful that I don't have to look up and decipher the stars at night. "The Heavens declare the glory of God; and the firmament shows His handiwork. Day unto day utters speech, and night unto night reveals knowledge," (Psalms 19:1-2). Remember, this is how the wise men were alerted to the birth of Jesus. They were directed by the star of the East. I enjoy stargazing and trying to identify the many constellations, but with all the light pollution and insufficient training regarding the stars, it can be difficult. Man's artificial light has drowned out God's speech, along with perverting it into horoscope readings, among other idolatrous monstrosities.

I'm so thankful I don't have to wait for instruction from a leader like Moses when he led the Israelites out of Egypt and through the wilderness for forty years. I praise God that I don't have to wait for a prophet to come to town for correction to be brought to my life. God already sent His only begotten Son Jesus, and then subsequently His Holy Spirit to connect with us personally. He also divinely instructed men to pen His words, which as Scripture tells us, are inspired by God. My Bible is one of my most prized possessions. It boggles my mind that God would choose to write a book that would be passed down from generation to generation, teaching us who He is and who we are as His beloved children.

I have heard from others that they didn't believe the Bible was true. If God can keep the earth on its 23.5-degree axis so we experience the four seasons, spinning at the perfect speed so we don't fall off and keep other planets and galaxies from bumping into us, I think He can keep His book intact. He is not a wimpy God. How extremely fortunate we are in this era to have not only the printed Word of God, but every human seems to have access to a cell phone connected to the internet. I remember being in some of the most remote places on earth and the people had cell phones. How convenient to have Bible apps on our phones downloaded with multiple translations right at our fingertips. In this country, we are certainly without excuse on Judgement Day for not spending time in the precious Word of God. You almost have to make a deliberate effort not to read the Word with all the alerts, daily devotionals, sermon videos and Bible studies so readily accessible to us without persecution from our families or government. Those freedoms can be stripped away faster than we think, and we should not take them for granted. Don't miss this opportunity to get to know the Lover of your soul, your Maker, our Father.

This book I felt led to write is certainly not for the faint of heart. It is a book full of how God is touching earth. The Creator of Heaven and earth loves us so much and He perfectly interacts with imperfect human beings who can be so temperamental, selfish and entitled. I know how easily I can get frustrated with myself, let alone mankind, yet this Almighty God gives us grace and mercy we don't deserve. I don't deserve it. It saddens me that one minute I can be thanking God, jumping up and down at His goodness, then seconds later the joy evaporates and my pride or selfishness creeps in so nonchalantly. He is giving you an invitation to say *yes* to Him today. Don't wait. If you have already surrendered to Jesus, I pray that my story has inspired you to look for Him in places that you may have overlooked. I pray you would be able to see that, even though the path is narrow, we are on it together with the One who is making diamonds out of us.

 Father, I invite You to be Lord and Savior of my life. I ask that You would guide me, give me wisdom and Your perfect peace. I surrender all to You this day, in Jesus' name.

THE END

You may contact me at Grow In Faith Ministries, Inc. at mike@ growinfaithministries.com for:

1. Women's Retreats and Conferences
2. Marriage Conferences along with my husband, Mike
3. Missions Mobilization
4. Restoring the Foundations Inner Healing Ministry